Squirreled Away

These squirrels just finished collecting acorns. Use the [clues]
to figure out how many acorns Twiggy found. Then fi[gure]
out how many acorns the squirrels collected altoget[her.]

Art by Valentina Mendicino Illustrations

Twiggy found 8 acorns.
The friends found 37 acorns altogether.

BONUS

Totally!

Ms. Digit's daughter loves to play with numbers. For fun today, she put together these lists. See if you can figure out which list gives you the largest answer. When you've got that, write the shaded letters from that list in order from right to left and top to bottom in the spaces below to find out Ms. Digit's daughter's first name.

1
- Number of Snow White's dw**A**rfs
- **M**inus the number of littl**E** pigs
- Multip**L**ied by the number of innings **I**n a regular major league baseball game
- Divided by **A** dozen

TOTAL: _____

2
- Number of days in Au**G**ust
- Minus the po**I**nts of a half-court basket in basketball
- Divide**D** by the number of quarts in a **G**allon
- Plus th**E** number of sides on an oc**T**agon

TOTAL: _____

3
- Age w**H**en you become **A** teenager
- Plus the **N**umber of letters in the alphabet
- Divided by the **N**umber of singers in **A** trio
- Minus the number of sides on a **H**exagon

TOTAL: _____

Ms. Digit's daughter's first name is ___ ___ ___ ___ ___ ___.

1. 7 − 3 = 4
4 × 9 = 36
36 ÷ 12 = 3

2. 31 − 3 = 28
28 ÷ 4 = 7
7 + 8 = 15

3. 13 + 26 = 39
39 ÷ 3 = 13
13 − 6 = 7

Ms. Digit's daughter's first name is **GIDGET**.

Stargazing

There should be **14** stars shining in these grids. Using the directions and hints below, can you figure out where all the stars go?

Look at the grids. Each numbered square tells you how many of the empty squares touching it (above, below, left, right, or diagonally) contain a star. Write an **X** on squares that can't have a star. Then write an **S** on squares that have a star.

HINTS:

- A star cannot go in a square that has a number.

- Even if you're not sure where to put all the stars around a number, fill in the ones you are sure of.

- Keep trying possibilities with a pencil and eraser!

This grid has 4 stars.

1			
2			1
		4	
1		3	

This grid has 10 stars.

	3		1		
					1
			2		2
	2	2	2		1
		2			
3				1	

I	X	X	X
2	S	X	I
X	S	4	S
I	X	3	S

S	3	X	I	X	X
S	S	X	X	S	I
X	X	2	S	X	2
X	2	2	2	S	I
S	S	2	X	X	X
3	S	X	X	I	S

Leaping Lemurs

These trees are loaded with lemurs! Every row of trees across, down, and diagonally has **30** lemurs in all. We've provided the exact number of lemurs hanging out in some of the trees. Can you figure out how many are on each of the other ones?

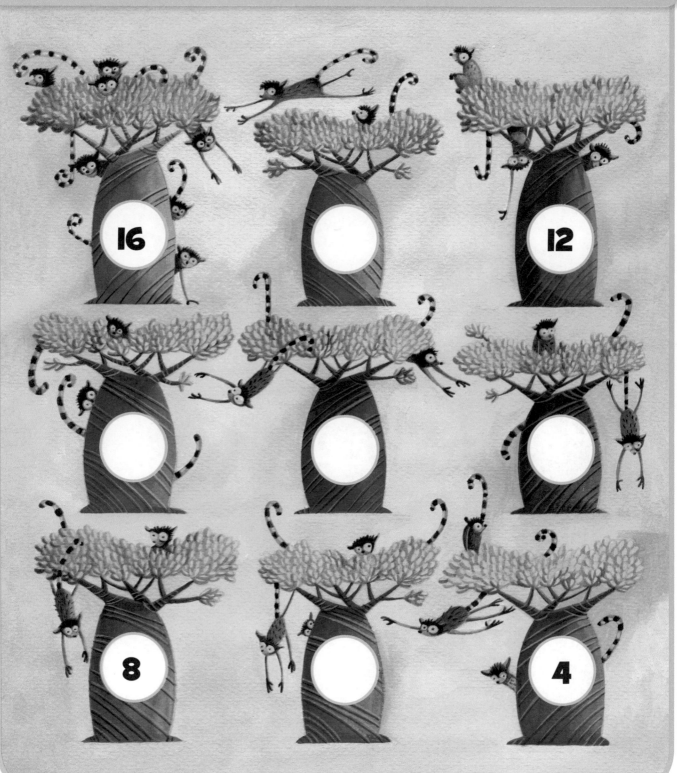

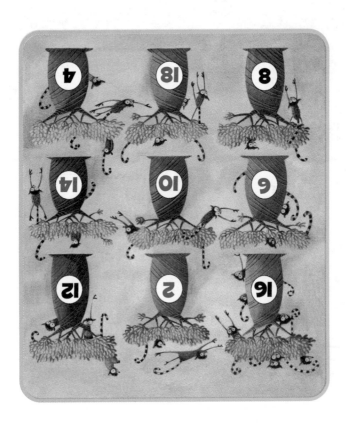

K-9 Academy

To solve these riddles, use the fractions of the words given below. The first one has been done for you.

Why was the dog excited to go to school?

Last ⅓ of BU**S**
First ½ of MEOW
Last ½ of PULL
Last ⅗ of SWING
First ¼ of BALL
Last ½ of TREE

The class was having a

S__ __ __ __ __ __ __ __ __ __ __ __ __ __ .

Why did the dog study before class?

First ⅓ of PURPLE
Last ¼ of JUMP
First ⅖ of QUEEN
Last ⅓ of SKI
First ⅕ of ZEBRA

In case the teacher gave a

__ __ __ __ __ __ __ __ __ __ .

BONUS: How many bones can you find in this scene?

Art by Josh Cleland

Why was the dog excited
to go to school?
The class was having a SMELLING BEE.

Why did the dog study before class?
In case the teacher gave a PUP QUIZ

BONUS
There are 36 bones.

Anita's Pitas

Anita Aardvark sells bags of pitas for **$4.00** per bag. After today's sales (listed below), how many bags of pitas did she sell? How much money did she make?

CLUES:

- Ruthie Rhino bought **12** bags.

- Hector Hippo paid **$12.00** for his bags.

- Ellie Elephant bought twice as many bags as Ruthie.

- Glen Giraffe paid **$28.00** less than Ellie paid.

BONUS
Anita lost her measuring cups. Can you find all **6** of them?

Art by Pat Lewis

Anita sold 56 bags of
pitas and made $224.00.

BONUS

One from the Heart

Help Jake uncover the secret message on his valentine. Match the numbers on the hearts to the spaces in the grid. Write each letter in its square to spell out the message. The numbers across the grid are on the right-hand side of the hearts, while the numbers down are on the left. Jake has already plotted his first heart.

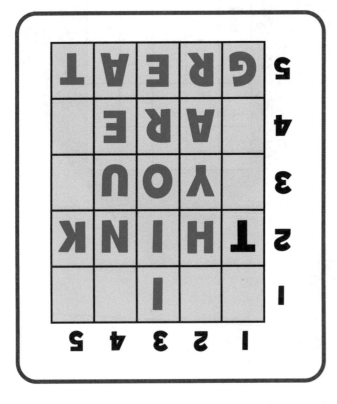

This Otter Be Fun

There should be **14** sea otters floating in this water. Using the directions and hints below, can you figure out where all the sea otters go?

Look at the grids. Each numbered square tells you how many of the empty squares touching it (above, below, left, right, or diagonally) contain a sea otter. Write an **X** on squares that can't have a sea otter. Then write **SO** on squares that have a sea otter.

HINTS:

- An otter cannot go in a square that has a number.

- Put an *X* on all the squares touching a zero.

- Even if you're not sure where to put all the otters connected to a number, fill in the ones you are sure of. (Look at what's not possible based on the other numbered squares. Try it with a pencil and eraser.)

This grid has 4 otters.

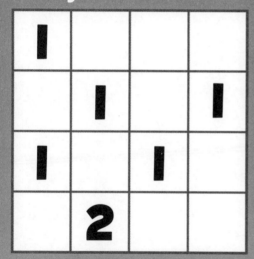

This grid has 10 otters.

Art by Sara Varon

os	os	X	X	X	os
os	4	X	2	X	1
X	X	os	os	X	X
1	X	os	4	X	1
os	X	X	X	X	os
1	X	0	X	os	2

X	os	2	os
X	1	X	1
X	1	X	1
os	X	os	1

In Good Shape

Can you tell which number belongs in each shape? Each number will always go inside the same shape. (Here's a clue: The number 7 goes in the pentagon, a five-sided shape.)

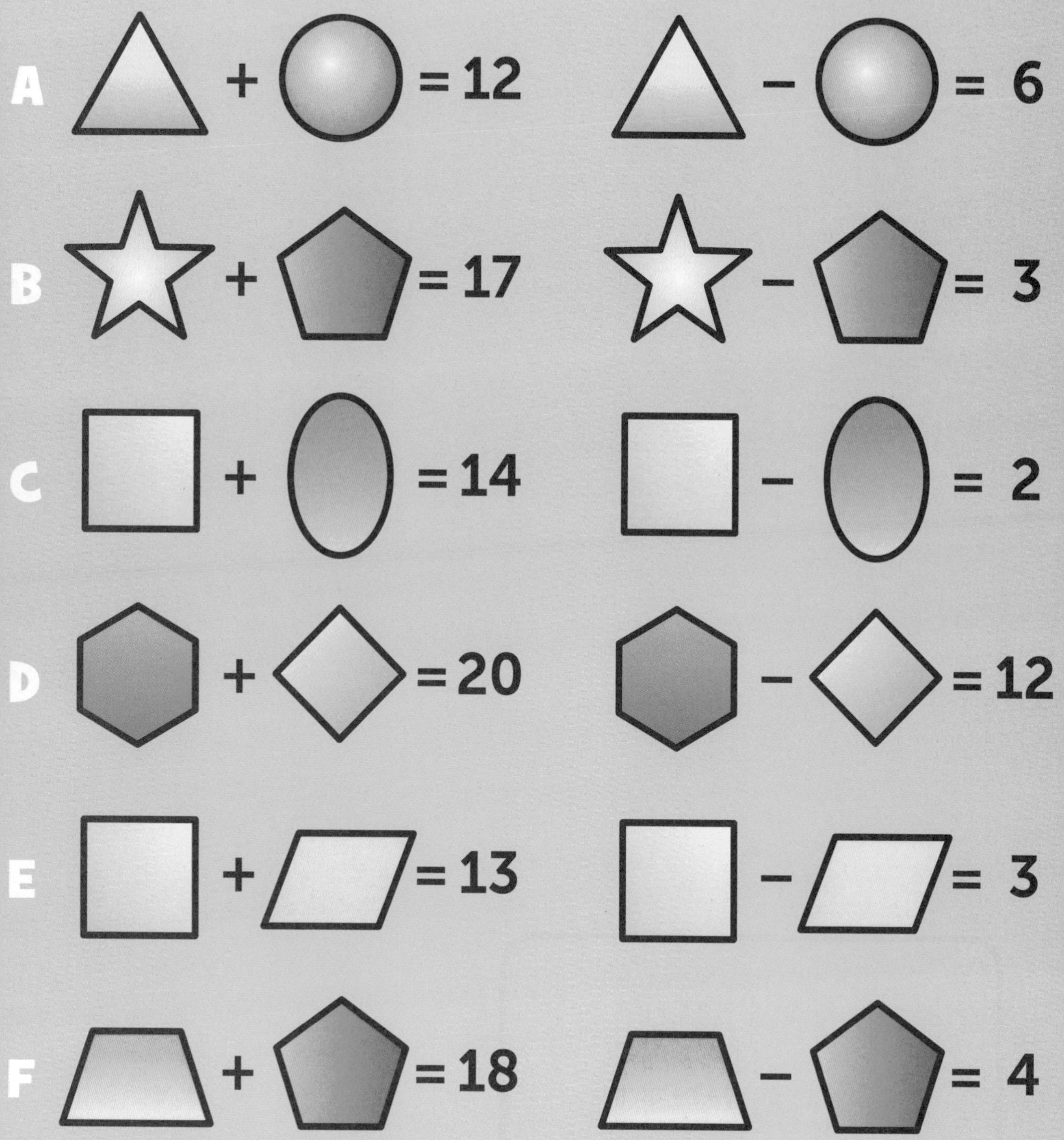

A △ + ● = 12   △ − ● = 6

B ★ + ⬠ = 17   ★ − ⬠ = 3

C ◻ + ⬭ = 14   ◻ − ⬭ = 2

D ⬡ + ◇ = 20   ⬡ − ◇ = 12

E ◻ + ▱ = 13   ◻ − ▱ = 3

F ▱ + ⬠ = 18   ▱ − ⬠ = 4

A. 9 + 3 = 12; 9 − 3 = 6
B. 10 + 7 = 17; 10 − 7 = 3
C. 8 + 6 = 14; 8 − 6 = 2
D. 16 + 4 = 20; 16 − 4 = 12
E. 8 + 5 = 13; 8 − 5 = 3
F. 11 + 7 = 18; 11 − 7 = 4

Divvy Up Desserts

Katie Cater is hosting a big Thanksgiving meal.
Can you help her sort the desserts?

Katie wants to rearrange the treats on the trays so that each of the red trays has the same number of cookies, each of the yellow trays has the same number of pumpkin-pie slices, and each of the orange trays has the same number of caramel apples. How many treats should be on each tray?

Katie Cater's cousins Ava, Brayden, and Carter made the desserts for their Thanksgiving gathering. Katie wants to write thank-you notes, but she can't remember which cousin brought each treat. Use the clues to help her figure out who made each dessert.

CLUES:

- Carter's dessert starts with the same letter as his name.

- Ava did not make cookies.

- Brayden's treat is served on a stick.

BONUS
Find **2** matching caramel apples.

Art by Josh Lewis

There should be 8 cookies on each red tray, 7 pumpkin-pie slices on each yellow tray, and 9 caramel apples on each orange tray.

THANKS FOR THE TREATS
Carter made cookies, Ava made pumpkin pie, and Brayden made caramel apples.

BONUS

Find Nine

To complete this grid, you must put a number from **1** to **9** into each empty space. No number can be repeated in any row (from side to side), any column (from top to bottom), or within any small square. We've filled in the numbers in the center square to help you get started.

	9	_	4	_	6	2	5	_
_	5	_	_	_	2	_	_	1
_	6	7	_	8	5	3	4	_
_	4	3	2	9	8	7	_	5
5	2	_	7	4	1	8	_	6
_	1	_	5	5	3	_	9	_
4	7	_	_	_	9	_	6	3
_	_	2	_	5	7	_	8	4
_	8	6	3	1	_	_	2	_

1	9	3	6	7	4	2	5	8
8	5	4	9	3	2	1	7	6
2	6	7	1	8	5	3	4	9
3	4	6	8	9	2	7	1	5
9	2	5	7	1	4	8	3	6
7	1	8	3	6	5	4	9	2
5	7	4	9	2	8	1	6	3
2	3	1	7	5	6	9	8	4
6	8	9	3	1	4	5	2	7

Monkeying Around

Each monkey at Monkey Manor is a different age. Moe, the youngest, is **7**. Maya, the second youngest, is **9**. Manuel is three times as old as Moe. Matilde is twice as old as Manuel. Mahir is four times as old as Maya. Marina is one-third the age of Mahir. Can you figure out the ages of Manuel, Matilde, Mahir, and Marina?

Manuel is 21 years old.
Matilde is 42 years old.
Mahir is 36 years old.
Marina is 12 years old.

Five Sides

Fitz's favorite number is **5**, and he has just finished drawing a maze with **5** sides. Help him get out of this perplexing pentagon. When you're done, see if you can spot **5** sets of **5** things in this scene.

START

FINISH

Art by Susan Miller

There are 5 flowers, squirrels, birds, ants
(by the garbage can), and pieces of chalk
(including the one in Fitz's hand).

Dozing Dinosaur

You can solve this riddle using the letters in the riddle itself. Just number the letters, left to right, from **1** to **26**. Then, write the letters in the spaces with their numbers. We filled in the first one to get you started: A is the 3rd letter in the riddle, so it goes in the space marked 3rd.

What dinosaur is a good sleeper?

A __ __ __ __ __ - __ __ __ __ __ - __ __
3rd 9th 4th 22nd 16th 8th 14th 7th 18th 26th 23rd 11th 20th

What dinosaur is a good sleeper?
A STEGO-SNORE-US

A Berry Special Puzzle

There should be **14** blueberries on these pancakes. Using the directions and hints below, can you figure out where all the blueberries go?

Look at the grids. Each numbered square tells you how many of the empty squares touching it (above, below, left, right, or diagonally) contain a blueberry. Write an **X** on squares that can't have a blueberry. Then write a **B** on squares that have a blueberry.

HINTS:

- A berry cannot go in a square that has a number.

- Put an *X* on all the squares touching a zero.

- Even if you're not sure where to put all the blueberries connected to a number, fill in the ones you are sure of.

- Remember how many blueberries you have to find for each puzzle.

This pancake has 4 blueberries.

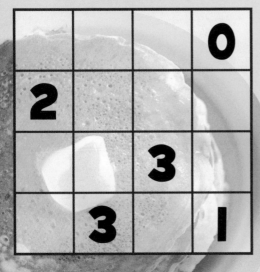

			0
2			
		3	
	3		1

This pancake has 10 blueberries.

	2		2	
				1
	3		6	
				1
	3		2	
2				1

Photos by Ryanjlane/iStock (pancakes); Rimblow/iStock (blueberries)

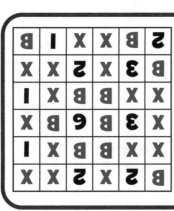

Zig Zag Zig

Can you place the numbers **1** through **9** in the circles on this page? Every number should appear in one circle. It looks easy enough, but there is a catch. Every arrow must point to a circle containing a greater number.

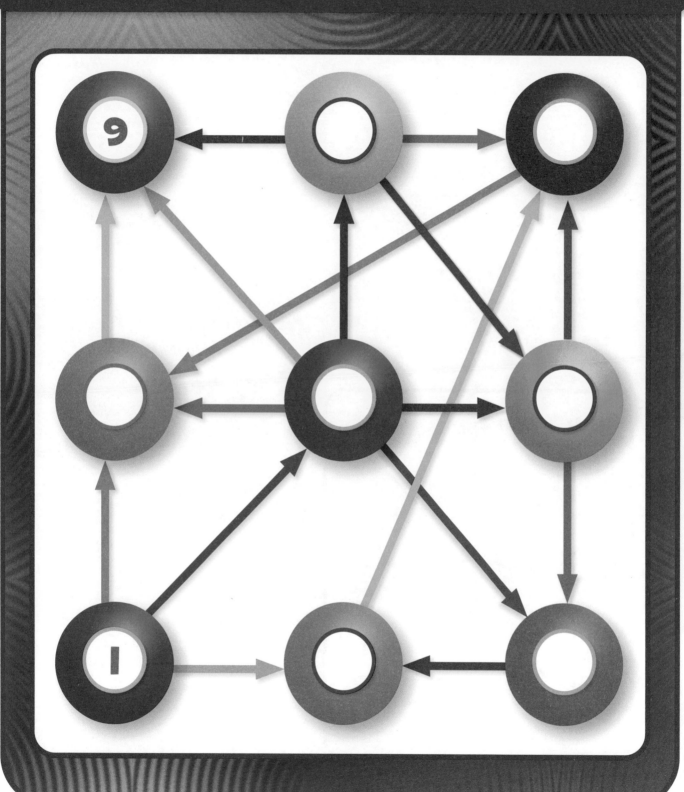

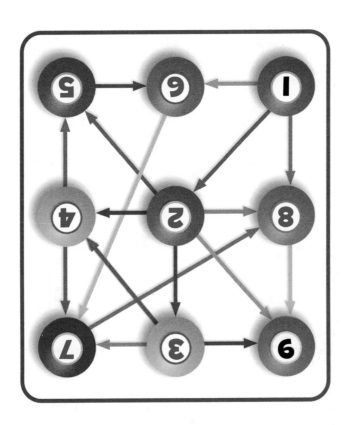

Run for Fun

Rocky, Rudy, and Ronnie are running in a **5**-mile race today to raise money for a local charity. Rocky ran at a speed of **5** miles per hour. Rudy ran at a rate of **10** minutes per mile. And Ronnie finished the race in **45** minutes. Who ran the fastest?

HINT:
Figure out how many minutes it took each to finish the race.

Rocky ran the race in 1 hour.
Rudy ran the race in 50 minutes.
Ronnie ran the race in 45 minutes.
Ronnie ran the fastest.

Milk Math

To solve this riddle, write the fractions of the words listed below in the blank spaces provided.

1. The first $\frac{1}{2}$ of KEYS

2. The first $\frac{3}{4}$ of EPIC

3. The first $\frac{2}{3}$ of TINSEL

4. The first $\frac{3}{4}$ of IDEA

5. The middle $\frac{3}{5}$ of OTHER

6. The middle $\frac{3}{5}$ of SCOWL

What's the best way to stop milk from going sour?

___ ___ ___ ___ ___   ___ ___ ___

___ ___ ___ ___ ___ ___ ___   ___ ___ ___ ___ .

Art by John Herzog

What's the best way to stop
milk from going sour?
KEEP IT INSIDE THE COW.

Going Bananas

To solve this puzzle, look at the pair of numbers under each blank. Find the first number along the orange row, and the second number along the blue column. Then find the banana where those two numbers meet. Write the letters you find in the blanks. We did the first one to get you started.

Why don't bananas get lonely?

T __ __ __   __ __ __ __ __ __   __ __ __ __
3,1 9,6 8,1 1,2   6,5 7,9 2,6 6,5 1,2 5,2   9,6 6,5 3,5 7,3

__ __ __ __ __ __   __ __   __ __ __ __ __ __ __ .
6,5 4,4 9,4 1,8 3,5 3,9   8,8 3,5   11,5 1,8 3,5 4,7 9,6 8,1 5,2

Art by Xiao Xin

Why don't bananas get lonely?
**THEY ALWAYS HANG
AROUND IN BUNCHES.**

Take Off!

Each row of planes below has a number pattern. For instance, as you move from one plane to the next in the first row, the numbers should all go up by three. But one plane in each row doesn't belong. Can you figure out which planes have the wrong numbers and what the correct numbers should be?

Row 1: 13 should be 14 (count up by 3).

Row 2: 56 should be 60 (count up by 5).

Row 3: 25 should be 23 (count up by 4).

Row 4: 5 should be 6 (count down by 1½).

Dinosaur Addition

Each dinosaur on this page has a value from **1** to **9**. No two dinosaurs have the same value.
Can you use the equations to figure out which number goes with which dinosaur?

HINT: = 1   = 9

1 + 1 = 2; 4 + 4 = 8
2 + 3 + 4 = 9
3 + 4 = 7; 7 + 2 = 9

$$\begin{array}{r} 11 \\ +22 \\ \hline 33 \end{array} \qquad \begin{array}{r} 35 \\ +21 \\ \hline 56 \end{array} \qquad \begin{array}{r} 47 \\ +12 \\ \hline 59 \end{array}$$

What's the Score?

Samantha, Taylor, and Aiden were playing basketball. Each person took **10** shots. Use the clues to figure out how many points each person scored. Each basket is worth **2** points.

CLUES:

- Half of Samantha's shots went in.

- Taylor scored twice as many baskets as Aiden.

- Aiden scored **4** points less than Samantha.

Art by Kelly Kennedy

Samantha scored 10 points.
Taylor scored 12 points.
Aiden scored 6 points.

Artful Addition

The total cost of the art supplies in each row and column is given.
Can you figure out the price of each item?

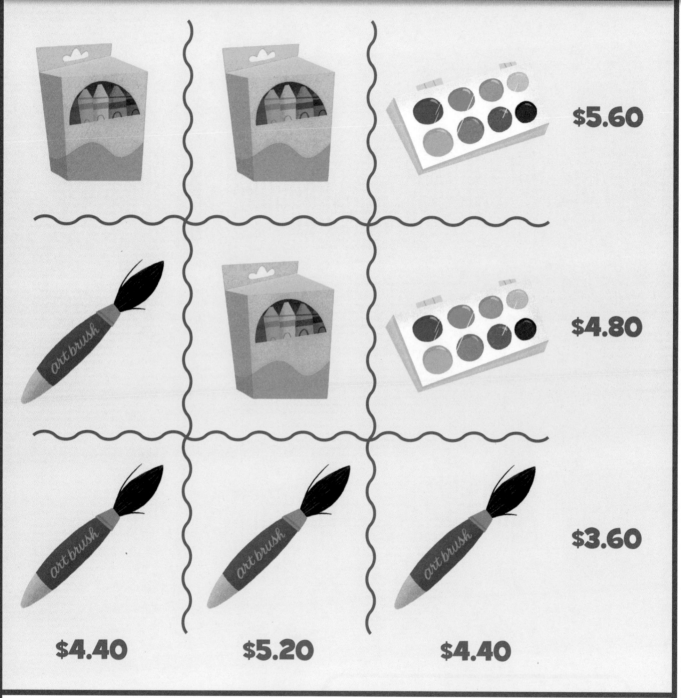

$5.60

$4.80

$3.60

$4.40

$5.20

$4.40

 = _____   = _____    = _____

Box of crayons = $2.00
Paintbrush = $1.20
Paints = $1.60

Penguin Pattern

The numbers on these penguins follow a pattern.
Figure out the pattern and then fill in the blanks.

START

1 5 4 8 7 11

SPLISH!

13 14 17

16 23 22

SPLASH!

29 25 32

Art by Robin Boyer

The pattern is +4, −1.
1, 5, 4, 8, 7, 11, 10, 14, 13, 17, 16,
20, 19, 23, 22, 26, 25, 29, 28, 32

Exactly Even

Can you find the path, using only even numbers, to get from IN to OUT?
You can move across, backward, up, or down, but not diagonally.

IN

23	8	16	41	3	99	49	61	33	99	51	39	55	21
19	5	14	10	96	88	32	39	91	10	17	41	9	83
15	55	33	96	79	35	40	11	13	18	33	93	91	37
14	41	51	49	91	85	6	98	42	14	38	26	24	23
16	28	14	6	72	81	21	5	19	7	43	2	9	87
2	65	21	35	8	10	14	20	16	51	17	18	17	99
50	17	22	13	35	79	37	63	94	39	14	26	89	21
58	20	26	66	24	88	21	5	92	11	51	64	81	57
67	18	53	62	77	14	7	5	80	61	7	82	46	20
5	69	21	5	57	16	11	39	76	33	81	93	59	38
96	28	30	84	24	70	9	55	12	4	18	26	50	56
71	13	33	20	41	7	19	11	15	63	7	39	61	99
75	21	57	12	14	28	56	34	44	56	90	20	41	7
17	61	73	33	85	89	21	93	13	85	95	6	87	39

OUT

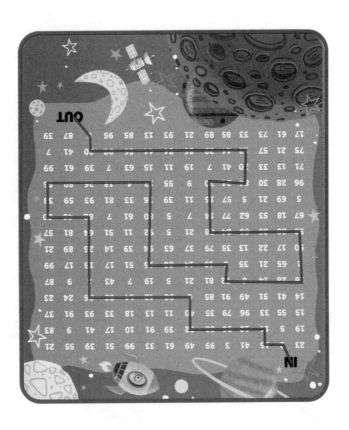

Words on the Web

Use the number pairs to solve the riddle on this page. Move to the right to the first number and then up to the second number. Write the letters you find in the correct spaces.

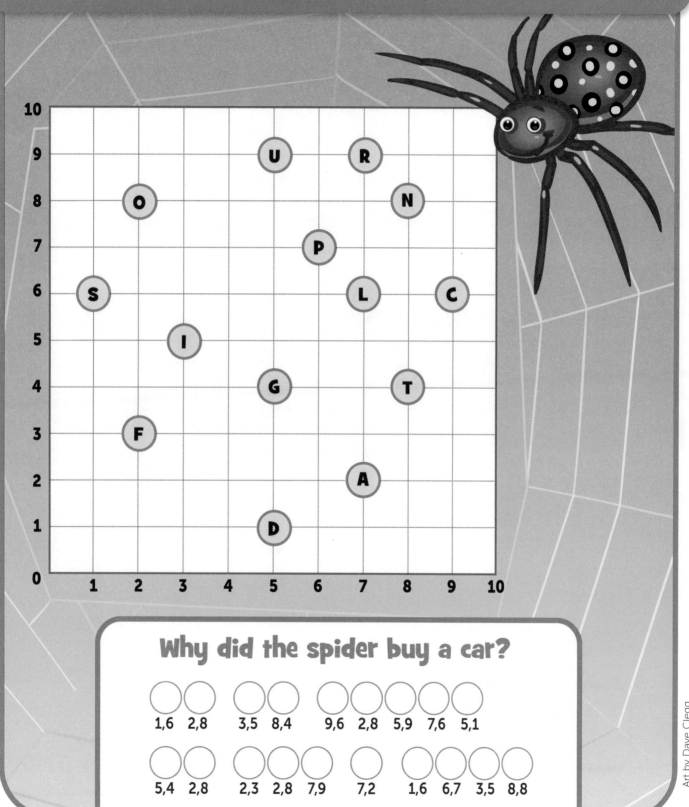

Why did the spider buy a car?

| 1,6 | 2,8 | | 3,5 | 8,4 | | 9,6 | 2,8 | 5,9 | 7,6 | 5,1 |

| 5,4 | 2,8 | | 2,3 | 2,8 | 7,9 | | 7,2 | | 1,6 | 6,7 | 3,5 | 8,8 |

Why did the spider buy a car?
SO IT COULD GO FOR A SPIN

Fish Frenzy

Newt works after school at the pet shop. His job is refilling the fishbowls on the shelves. Each type of fish has its own bowl. When Newt is finished, every row up and down, across, and diagonally will have **15** total fish. Can you figure out where each fish goes?

Take a Guesstimate

The students in Mr. Count's class have made their guesses about the number of items in each of the jars below. Mr. Count was about to determine the winners when the answer slips got mixed up. Look at the jars and use the clues to figure out which number of items goes with each jar.

CLUES:

- The popcorn kernels are the tiniest items.

- The toy cars are the largest items.

- There are fewer mints than marbles.

- There are more pieces of bow-tie pasta than marbles.

136 53 108 320 9

There are 136 pieces of bow-tie pasta, 9 toy cars, 108 marbles, 320 popcorn kernels, and 53 mints.

Make a Move

Mr. and Mrs. Melody are planning to move into a new house. Mr. Melody is a music teacher and goes to the school **5** days a week. Mrs. Melody manages a music shop and works **6** days a week. Which house should they choose if they want to travel the fewest total miles to and from work each week?

HOUSE 1 = 112 miles per week.
HOUSE 2 = 110 miles per week.
HOUSE 3 = 74 miles per week.
HOUSE 4 = 116 miles per week.

Mr. and Mrs. Melody should move to House 3 to travel the fewest miles each week.

Getting Antsy

There should be **14** ants hiding in this picnic tablecloth. Using the directions and hints below, can you figure out where all the ants go?

Look at the grids. Each numbered square tells you how many of the empty squares touching it (above, below, left, right, or diagonally) contain an ant. Write an **X** on squares that can't have an ant. Then write an **A** on squares that have an ant.

This grid has 4 ants.

			2
1		2	
	1		1

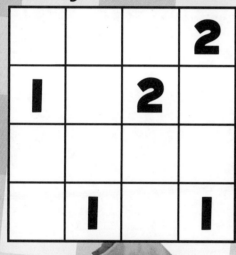

This grid has 10 ants.

2			2		
		5			1
3			0		2
	1				
1			1		2

Photo by © Jules Frazier/Exactostock-1598/SuperStock

A	X	A	2
1	X	2	A
X	X	X	X
X	1	A	1

2	A	A	2	X	X
X	A	5	A	X	1
A	A	X	X	X	A
3	X	X	0	X	2
A	1	X	X	X	A
1	X	X	1	A	2

Candy Counter

Each piece of colorful candy costs less than ten cents. Can you look at these equations and figure out the price of each kind?

$$5 + 5 + 5 + 5 + 5 = 25$$
$$9 + 9 = 9 + 9$$
$$7 - 7 + 7 + 7 = 14$$
$$18 - 6 - 6 = 6$$
$$8 + 8 + 8 + 8 = 24 + 8$$
$$14 - 2 - 2 - 2 - 2 = 6$$
$$4 + 4 + 6 - 2 = 4 + 8$$
$$3 + 3 + 3 = 12 - 3$$

Missing Microphone

Tonight is the Crittertown Talent Show. But Allie Gator can't find her lucky microphone! She suspects it was accidentally taken from backstage between **7:00** and **7:09**, while she was changing in the dressing room. The other performers all had access to the backstage area. Use the clues to figure out which performer could have taken the microphone between **7:00** and **7:09**.

CLUES:

- Bella Phant practiced her four songs in a practice room starting at **6:30**. Each song took **11** minutes to practice.

- Howie Wolfer spent **10** minutes practicing his scales and **10** minutes rehearsing his song. He started practicing **19** minutes after Bella Phant started.

- Red Bird practiced her violin **15** minutes more than Bella Phant practiced, but she started **9** minutes later.

- Gerry Raffe finished practicing his cello **40** minutes before Red Bird finished practicing.

BONUS
How many hidden music notes can you find?

Art by Mike Moran

Gerry Raffe finished practicing at 6:58.
He could have taken the microphone
between 7:00 and 7:09.

BONUS

Robot Vacation

Cross out all the boxes in which the number can be evenly divided by **3**.
Then write the leftover letters in the spaces to spell the answer.

33	31	9	17	13	42	8	27	10	39	91
H	T	R	O	R	Q	E	Z	C	A	H

24	54	37	55	12	2	60	11	18	23	77
B	Y	A	R	L	G	W	E	M	H	I

30	43	36	22	35	90	3	38	21	5	99
F	S	N	B	A	E	O	T	K	T	S

81	18	43	45	53	15	28	46	54	6	19
D	V	E	C	R	J	I	E	P	B	S

Why did the robot go on vacation?

___ ___   ___ ___ ___ ___ ___ ___ ___ ___

___ ___ ___   ___ ___ ___ ___ ___ ___ ___

Why did the robot go on vacation?
TO RECHARGE HIS BATTERIES

Order in the Court

Judge J. J. Jones Jr. needs some order in her courtroom.
You can help by figuring out what number comes next in each series.
Hurry, before she has to pound her gavel again!

A 2, 4, 7, 11, __16__

B 12, 10, 6, _____

C 5, 10, 20, _____

D 27, 9, 3, _____

E 24, 12, 6, _____

F 4, 8, 16, _____

G 8, 12, 18, _____

H 60, 50, 35, _____

I 6000, 600, 60, _____

J 50, 100, 200, _____

K 1, 5, 25, 125, _____

L 5, 9, 7, 11, 9, _____

M 2, 4, 16, _____

N 18, 6, 36, 12, 72, _____

O 50, 100, 10, 20, 2, _____

P 120, 60, 30, _____

Q 24, 28, 20, 24, _____

R 30, 10, 60, 20, _____

S 15, 30, 34, 68, 72, _____

T 6, 12, 9, 15, 12, _____

Art by Jim Paillot

A.	16	Each adds 1 more
B.	0	Subtract increments of 2
C.	40	Double the preceding number
D.	1	Divide each by 3
E.	3	Take away half
F.	32	Double the preceding number
G.	26	Add sequence of even numbers
H.	15	Subtract increments of 5
I.	6	Divide each by 10
J.	400	Double the preceding number
K.	625	Multiply each by 5
L.	13	Add 4, then subtract 2
M.	256	Multiply each number by itself
N.	24	Divide by 3, then multiply by 6
O.	4	Multiply by 2, then divide by 10
P.	15	Divide each by 2
Q.	16	Add 4, then subtract 8
R.	120	Divide by 3, then multiply by 6
S.	144	Multiply by 2, then add 4
T.	18	Add 6, then subtract 3

Two Steps

Can you find your way through this maze of numbers from START to FINISH? To find the right path, you must add or subtract **2** each time to find the next box. You must pass through every box in the maze once. You may move horizontally or vertically, but not diagonally.

START

FINISH

Art by Paul Richer

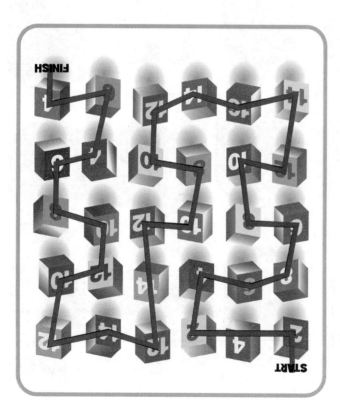

Dill in the Blanks

There should be **14** pickle slices on these sandwiches. Using the directions and hints below, can you figure out where all the pickles go?

Look at the grids. Each numbered square tells you how many of the empty squares touching it (above, below, left, right, or diagonally) contain a pickle. Write an **X** on squares that can't have a pickle. Then write a **P** on squares that have a pickle.

This grid has 4 pickles.

1	2	1	
2	4	2	

This grid has 10 pickles.

0			4		1
	1				2
			1		
	2				
2			2		3

Photos by Suzifoo/iStock (pickles); Kyoshino (plate); BWFolsom/iStock (sandwich)

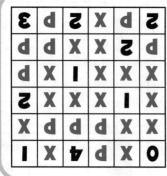

Lunch at The Banana Café

Max is meeting his friends for lunch at The Banana Café. If he chooses one appetizer, one main dish, and one dessert, what can he order that will cost exactly **$10.00**? How many combinations can you find?

Appetizers

Banana Smoothie	$2.50
Banana Bread	$2.00
Banana Fritter	$3.00
Banana Crêpe	$3.75

Main Dishes

Grilled Banana Sandwich	$4.25
Banana Tacos	$3.00
BBQ Bananas	$5.50
Banana Fruit Salad	$4.00

Desserts

Frozen Bananas	$2.00
Banana Split	$3.25
Banana Cream Pie	$4.00
Banana Custard Cupcake	$2.75

BONUS BANANA CHALLENGE

Each of Max's friends is planning to order a different dessert.
Use the clues below to figure out who will eat what.

- Monte would like the most expensive dessert. _____

- Millie had a banana smoothie for an appetizer, so she doesn't want to order anything frozen for dessert. _____

- Miko's dessert costs $1.25 more than Mei's dessert. _____

Max could order Banana Bread, a Banana Fruit Salad, and a Banana Cream Pie.

He could also order a Banana Fritter, a Grilled Banana Sandwich, and a Banana Custard Cupcake.

What other combinations did you find?

BONUS BANANA CHALLENGE
Mei: Frozen Bananas
Miko: Banana Split
Monte: Banana Cream Pie
Millie: Banana Custard Cupcake

Time Find

Every clock time can be written as a number. For example, **3** o'clock can be written as **3:00**. Write the numbers for the times shown on each clock. Then try to find those times in the grid. The times might be found up, down, across, backward, or diagonally.

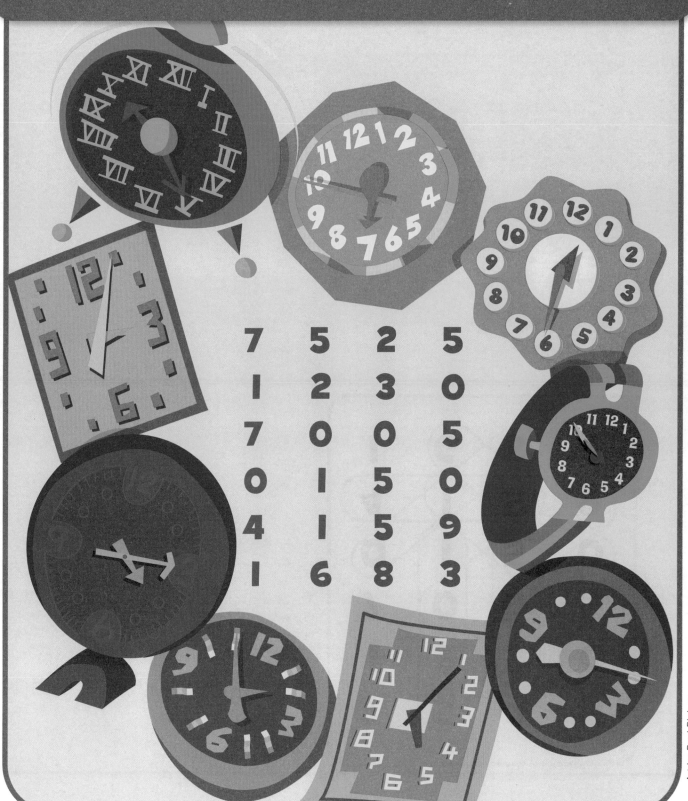

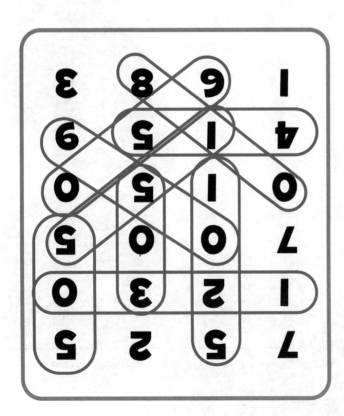

Frozen Fun

Solve these problems as you snowboard down the mountain. Then write the matching letters in the spaces at the bottom to finish the riddle. Some letters will be used more than once.

C

$6 \times ? = 12$

E

$7 \times ? = 21$

I

$5 \times ? = 5$

P

$9 \times ? = 54$

R

$4 \times ? = 16$

S

$8 \times ? = 40$

What do snowmen eat for breakfast?

____ ____ ____   ____ ____ ____ ____ ____ ____ ____ ____
 1   2   3   2   4   1   5   6   1   3   5

What do snowmen eat for breakfast?
ICE CRISPIES

Math Mirth

Do some math, then get a laugh! Use the fractions of the words listed below to solve the two riddles given in this puzzle.

1. What is a math teacher's favorite dessert?

P _ _ _ _ _ _ _ _ _

First ⅓ of **PIG**
First ½ of **UMPIRE**
First ¾ of **KING**
First ⅓ of **PILLOW**

2. Which knight helped King Arthur build his round table?

S I _ _ _ _ _ _ _ _ _ _

First ⅔ of **SIT**
Last ⅔ of **ARC**
Last ½ of **PLUM**
First ½ of **FERRET**
Last ½ of **SENTENCE**

What is a math teacher's
favorite dessert?
PUMPKIN PI

Which knight helped King Arthur
build his round table?
SIR CUMFERENCE

Prairie Pop-Up

There should be **14** prairie dogs hidden in the grass. Using the directions and hints below, can you figure out where all the prairie dogs go?

Look at the grids. Each numbered square tells you how many of the empty squares touching it (above, below, left, right, or diagonally) contain a prairie dog. Write an **X** on squares that can't have a prairie dog. Then write **PD** on squares that have a prairie dog.

This grid has 4 prairie dogs.

0			2
	4		
			1
2		1	

This grid has 10 prairie dogs.

1		0			
				4	
4		3			
					1
3		1			
				1	

pp	I	X	X	X	pp
X	X	X	I	X	3
X	I	X	pp	pp	X
X	X	pp	3	pp	4
pp	4	X	X	pp	X
pp	pp	X	0	X	I

X	I	X	2
I	X	pp	pp
X	4	pp	X
2	pp	X	0

Flower Addition

Each flower on this page has a value from **1** to **9**. No two flowers have the same value.
Can you use the equations to figure out which number goes with which flower?

 + **=**

——— ——— ———

 + **=**

——— ——— ———

 + **+** **=**

——— ——— ——— ———

 + **=**

——— ——— ———

 + **=**

——— ——— ———

——— ———

+

——— ———

———

+

———

———

+

———

HINT: 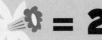 **= 2**   **= 8**

Art by Mike Moran

2 + 6 = 8; 3 + 3 = 6

3 + 2 + 2 = 7

2 + 5 = 7; 6 + 3 = 9

$$\begin{array}{r}11\\+66\\\hline 77\end{array}\qquad\begin{array}{r}12\\+52\\\hline 64\end{array}\qquad\begin{array}{r}43\\+55\\\hline 98\end{array}$$

Poppy's Copies

Poppy Okapi had a sale at her photocopy business. Copies cost **10** cents per sheet of paper. How much did each of today's customers pay?

1. Myna Byrd made **33** copies of her short poem "Byrds of a Feather" to give to friends.

2. Don Key made **40** copies of a flyer for the community-theater production of *Home of the Bray*.

3. Al Paca made **2** dozen copies of his flyer for the annual neighborhood yard sale.

4. Bob Catt made **3** copies of his 16-page book *Catt Tales*.

BONUS
One pack of paper has **100** sheets. If Poppy started the day with **2** packs of paper, how many sheets did she have left after the day's sales?

Art by Madeline Cohen

1. $3.30 **3.** $2.40
2. $4.00 **4.** $4.80

BONUS
Poppy had 55 sheets of paper left.

Similar Circles

Can you tell which circle doesn't belong?

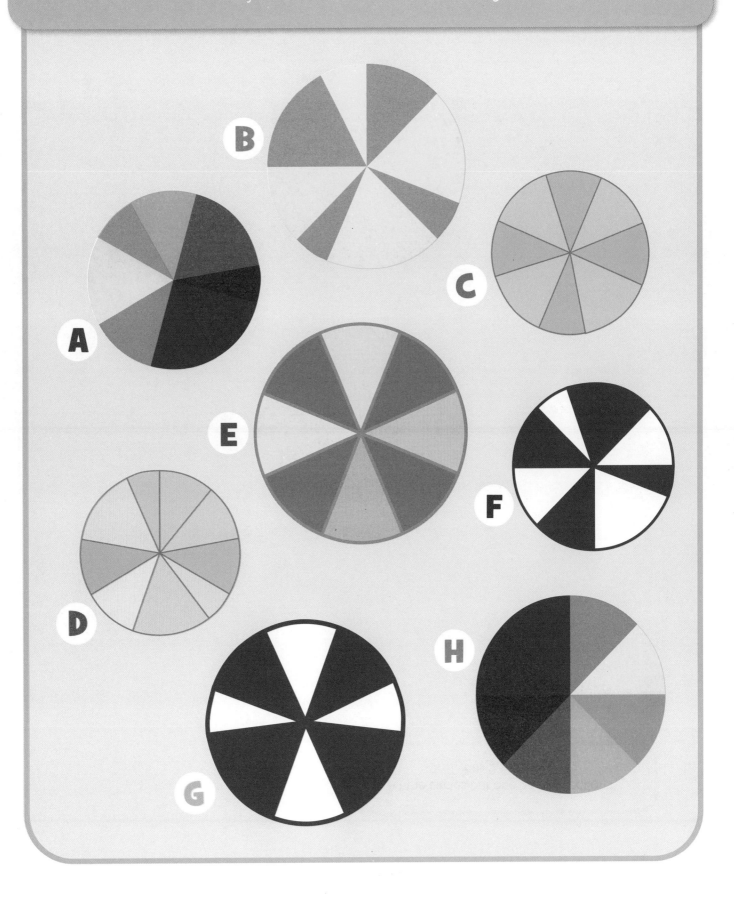

All the circles but one have 8 sections.
D has 9 sections.

Matrix 60

One of the rows, columns, or diagonals of this matrix has five numbers that, when added together, total **60**. Which one is it?

Art by Olga Skomorokhova

					53
1	18	2	16	24	=61
6	14	19	15	7	=61
23	11	0	8	20	=62
21	9	13	17	3	=63
5	10	22	4	12	=53
=	=	=	=	=	
56	62	56	60	66	44

Minus Maze

Help this bee find its way to its hive! Start by subtracting the first pair of numbers (**6 - 1**). Draw a line to the answer (**5**), then move to the next pair of numbers and do the same. Answers may be to the left, right, up, or down.

START

6 - 1	5	3 - 3	0	6 - 2	6	6 - 5	1	3 - 1
7		6		4		3		5
4 - 2	6	2 - 1	3	4 - 1	4	6 - 4	2	2 - 2
2		1		5		6		0
5 - 3	9	6 - 3	6	5 - 2	3	7 - 1	5	7 - 3
2		3		0		8		4
2 - 2	4	5 - 5	4	4 - 4	6	8 - 2	4	3 - 1
6		0		1		4		2
7 - 2	7	8 - 1	0	3 - 3	6	5 - 1	3	4 - 2
5		9		6		8		2
3 - 2	1	7 - 7	0	6 - 5	1	9 - 1	9	FINISH

Art by Jannie Ho

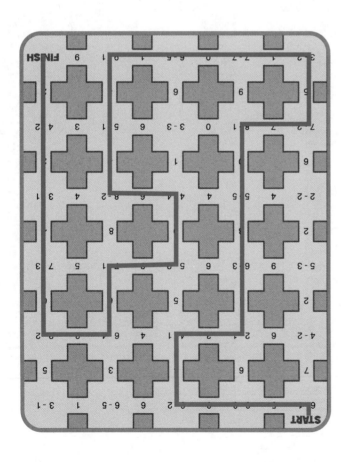

Farm Find

Can you find the five farm animals hiding behind this barn? First solve all the math problems. Then find the numbers in each equation in the grid. Put the letters matching the numbers in the correct spaces under each equation.

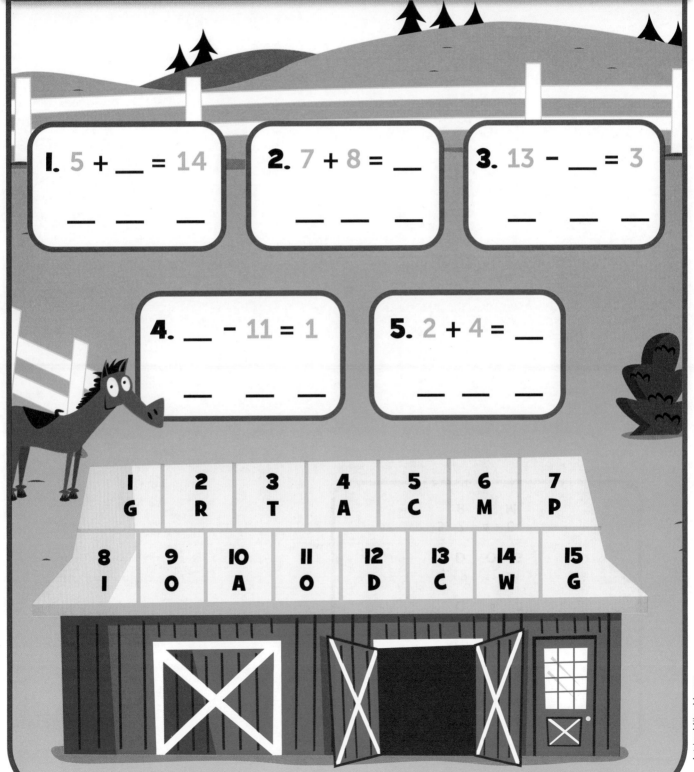

1. $5 + \_\_ = 14$

_ _ _

2. $7 + 8 = \_\_$

_ _ _

3. $13 - \_\_ = 3$

_ _ _

4. $\_\_ - 11 = 1$

_ _ _

5. $2 + 4 = \_\_$

_ _ _

1	2	3	4	5	6	7
G	R	T	A	C	M	P

8	9	10	11	12	13	14	15
I	O	A	O	D	C	W	G

Art by Mike Moran

1. 5 + 9 = 14
C O W

2. 7 + 8 = 15
P I G

3. 13 − 10 = 3
C A T

4. 12 − 11 = 1
D O G

5. 2 + 4 = 6
R A M

Bike Times

Arnie, Angel, Alex, and Alisha are riding their bicycles on a **60**-mile trip, all the way to Narrowsburg. Each leaves at a different time, but all of them arrive in Narrowsburg at **1:00 p.m.** Can you tell how fast (in miles per hour) each biker pedaled? First, figure out how many hours it took each biker to reach Narrowsburg. Then divide the distance by the hours.

DEPARTURE TIMES

- Arnie left at 7:00 a.m.

- Angel left at 8:00 a.m.

- Alex left at 9:00 a.m.

- Alisha left at 10:00 a.m.

Arnie biked at 10 miles per hour.
Angel biked at 12 miles per hour.
Alex biked at 15 miles per hour.
Alisha biked at 20 miles per hour.

Bingo!

To find the winning row of numbers on this bingo card, first solve all the problems in the colored circles. Then cross off the numbers on the card that match the answers.

23 − 4 ____

90 ÷ 3 ____

59 + 5 ____

3 x 7 ____

28 + 13 ____

64 − 5 ____

7 x 5 ____

69 ÷ 3 ____

65 + 9 ____

41 − 12 ____

83 − 12 ____

9 ÷ 9 ____

26 ÷ 2 ____

2 x 5 ____

39 + 8 ____

43 − 9 ____

34 + 9 ____

69 − 6 ____

15 + 13 ____

6 x 6 ____

6 x 8 ____

14 ÷ 7 ____

3 + 4 ____

45 + 6 ____

5 x 3 ____

8 ÷ 2 ____

B	I	N	G	O
11	18	38	47	64
9	22	39	58	70
13	29	X	49	67
4	27	37	56	75
1	23	36	51	63

Ice Team

The Powerful Pros just won the championship! One teammate was named Most Valuable Player. Use the players' jersey numbers to figure out who the MVP is.

CLUES:

- The sum of the two digits is either **8** or **9**.

- If you switch the order of the digits, the new number would be **18** greater than it is now.

The MVP is number 35.

Three's a Crowd

Cross out all the boxes in which the number cannot be evenly divided by **3**. Then write the leftover letters in the spaces to spell the answer.

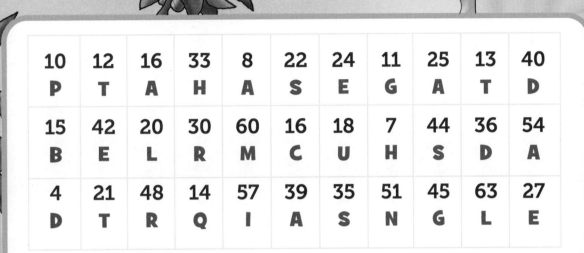

10	12	16	33	8	22	24	11	25	13	40
P	T	A	H	A	S	E	G	A	T	D

15	42	20	30	60	16	18	7	44	36	54
B	E	L	R	M	C	U	H	S	D	A

4	21	48	14	57	39	35	51	45	63	27
D	T	R	Q	I	A	S	N	G	L	E

Where did the Three Musketeers go on vacation?

___ ___ _____ _____

Where did the Three Musketeers
go on vacation?
THE BERMUDA TRIANGLE

Caterpillar Pattern

The numbers on this caterpillar follow a pattern.
Figure out the pattern and then fill in the blanks.

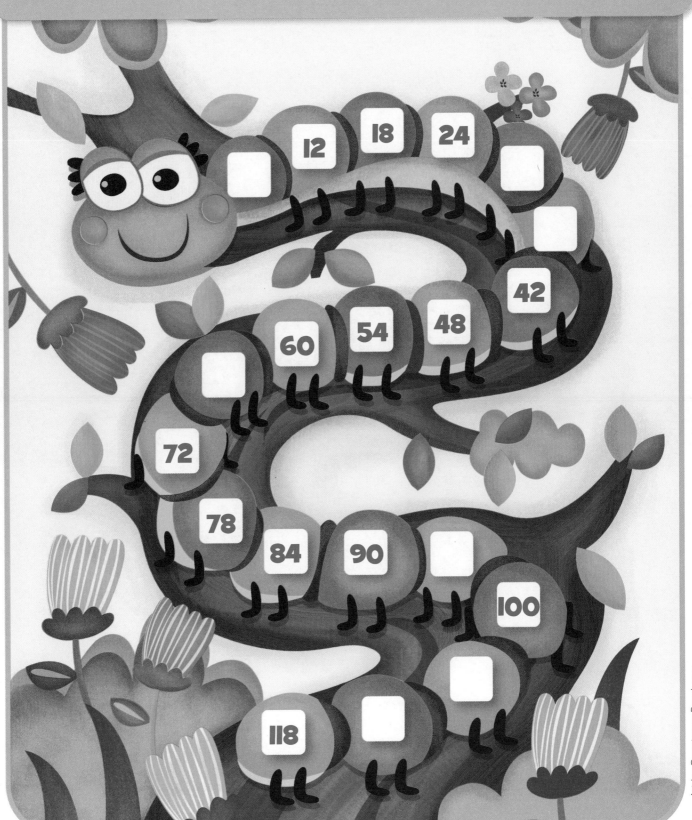

Art by Constanza Basaluzzo

The numbers go up by 6.
6, 12, 18, 24, 30, 36, 42, 48, 54, 60, 66, 72,
78, 84, 90, 96, 100, 106, 112, 118

Flying Numbers

Each kite stands for a number. Use the kite key to figure out the punch lines to the number jokes below.

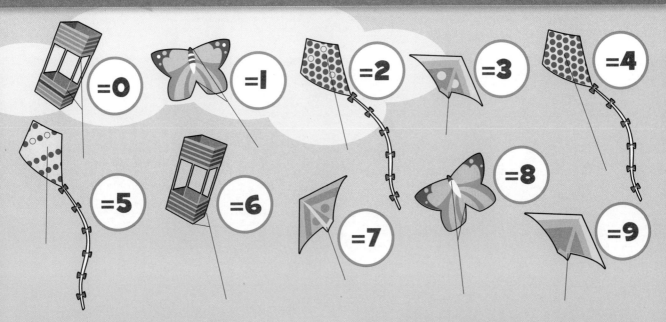

=0 =1 =2 =3 =4

=5 =6 =7 =8 =9

Why was 6 mad at 7?

Because

Why is a circle always so hot?

Because it's  °

What does a dollar have in common with the moon?

They both have

quarters.

How does 10 feel without its number 1 friend?

Like a

What happened when 19 and 20 got into an argument?

[kite images]

How do numbers celebrate?

With high [kite] 's

Why was 6 mad at 7?
BECAUSE 789

Why is a circle always so hot?
BECAUSE IT'S 360°

What does a dollar have in common
with the moon?
THEY BOTH HAVE 4 QUARTERS.

How does 10 feel without
its number 1 friend?
LIKE A 0

What happened when 19 and 20 got
into an argument?
21

How do numbers celebrate?
WITH HIGH 5'S

Total Turkeys

These gobblers have been "weighting" to meet you. Can you
find three turkeys whose weights total exactly **50** pounds?
You will need to use one bird from each row.

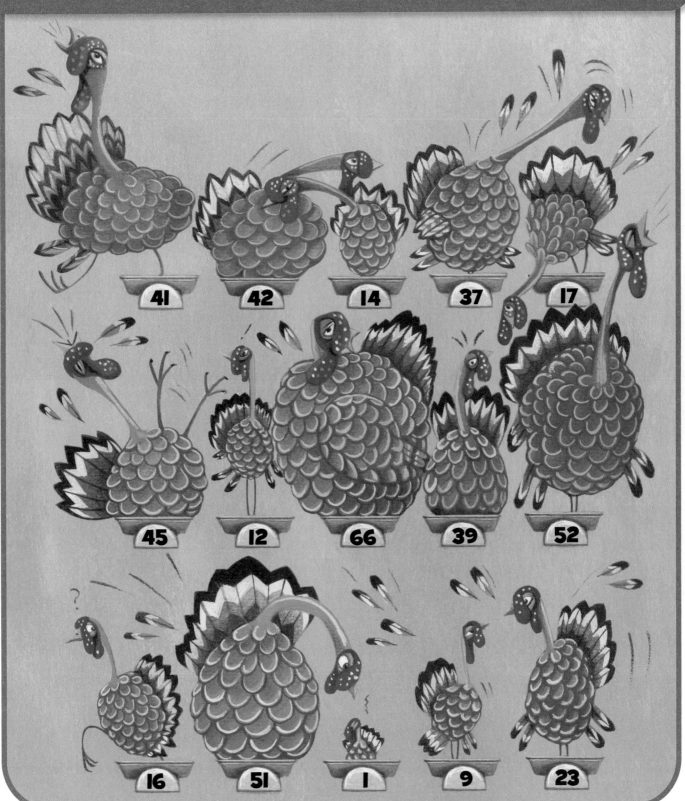

41 42 14 37 17

45 12 66 39 52

16 51 1 9 23

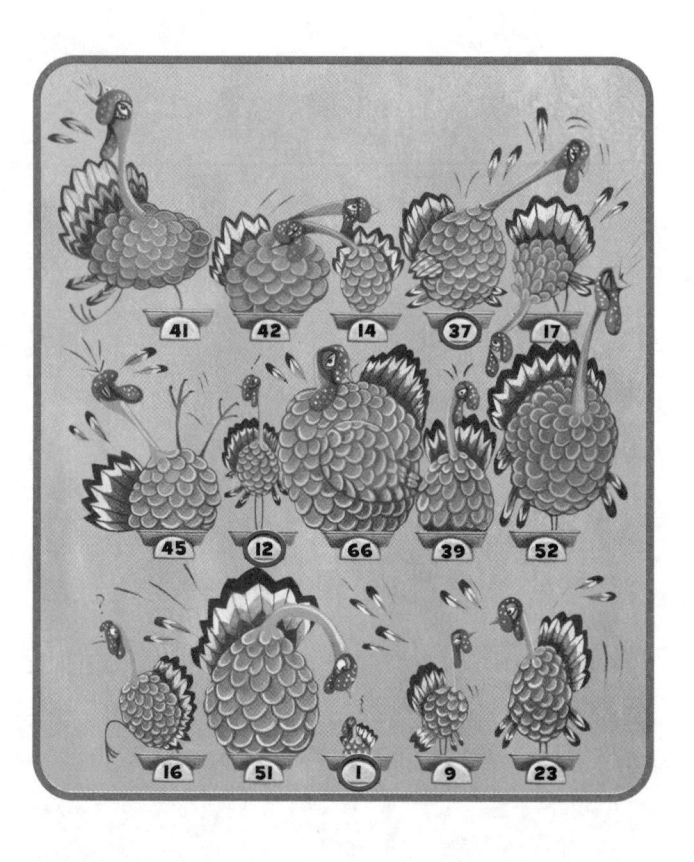

Sally's Sea-Store Super Sale

Sally's Sea Store is having its annual summertime super sale. Rey wants to buy one pair of sandals and one pair of sunglasses. Can you help her find the best deal?

Art by Pat Lewis

Best deal: Buy the green sunglasses and get a pair of sandals free for a total cost of $20.00.

Jump to Conclusions

Brenda, Burgundy, and Brielle are playing a jump-rope game in which each player chants the alphabet while jumping, calling out one letter for every jump. They get one point for every letter completed. The list below shows each jumper's last completed letter for each turn. Can you figure out who won the game?

JUMPER	TURN 1	TURN 2	TURN 3	TURN 4
Brenda	J	M	P	L
Burgundy	Q	N	F	K
Brielle	L	L	J	O

Art by Julissa Mora

Brenda had 51 points and won
(10 + 13 + 16 + 12 = 51).

Burgundy had 48 points
(17 + 14 + 6 + 11 = 48).

Brielle had 49 points
(12 + 12 + 10 + 15 = 49).

To the Hoop!

Cross out all the boxes in which the number can be evenly divided by **3**. Then write the leftover letters in the spaces to spell the answer.

10	33	5	20	12	8	21	16	25	41	3
T	I	H	E	C	Y	N	R	E	A	W

13	9	37	24	19	52	36	14	38	6	40
L	E	W	K	A	Y	M	S	D	F	R

99	7	50	30	26	35	15	4	23	60	11
G	I	B	D	B	L	V	I	N	Y	G

Why are basketball players messy eaters?

_ _ _ _ ' _ _ _ _ _ _ _ _

_ _ _ _ _ _ _ _ _ _ .

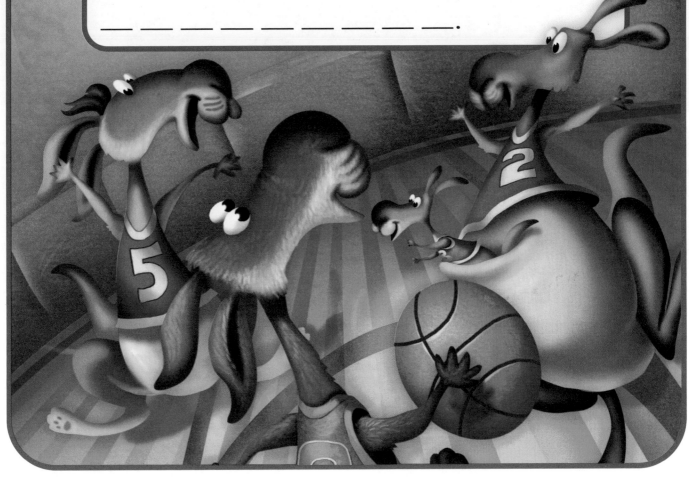

Why are basketball players
messy eaters?
THEY'RE ALWAYS DRIBBLING.

Holey Moley

There should be **13** holes in these slices of Swiss cheese. Using the directions and hints below, can you figure out where all the holes go?

Look at the grids. Each numbered square tells you how many of the empty squares touching it (above, below, left, right, or diagonally) contain a Swiss cheese hole. Write an **X** on squares that can't have a hole. Then write an **H** on squares that have a hole.

HINTS:

- Put an *X* on all the squares touching a zero.

- Look at the sides of the big grid, where large numbers may make it more obvious where Swiss cheese holes are located.

- A cheese hole cannot go in a square that has a number.

This grid has 3 Swiss cheese holes.

			1
0		2	
			1
	2		

This grid has 10 Swiss cheese holes.

		2			2
2				2	4
	1				
					1
	3		3		

X	X	H	I
0	X	2	X
X	X	H	I
H	2	X	X

X	2	X	X	2	X
H	H	X	X	H	H
2	X	X	2	H	4
X	I	X	X	X	H
X	X	H	H	X	I
H	3	H	3	X	X

Two-Twos!

At the Twirly Two-Two Dance Studio, students love two things: tutus and math! Help them dance through their latest math challenge. Each row in the square below includes five number 2s. Use addition, subtraction, multiplication, or division signs between the 2s to come up with the answer at the end of each row.

HINT:
Here's one way to solve the first row's equation:
$2 - 2 \times 2 \times 2 \times 2 = 0$.

2   2   2   2   2 = 0
2   2   2   2   2 = 1
2   2   2   2   2 = 2
2   2   2   2   2 = 3
2   2   2   2   2 = 4
2   2   2   2   2 = 5

Art by Mike Herrod

Here are our answers.
You may have found others.

$2 - 2 \times 2 \times 2 \times 2 = 0$
$2 + 2 + 2 \div 2 - 2 = 1$
$2 \times 2 - 2 + 2 - 2 = 2$
$2 \div 2 + 2 + 2 - 2 = 3$
$2 + 2 \times 2 - 2 - 2 = 4$
$2 + 2 + 2 \div 2 + 2 = 5$

Garden Plotting

The squares below show the garden plots of Mouse, Mole, Squirrel, and Rabbit. Look at each friend's sections of lettuce and tomatoes. Then answer the questions.

1. Which friend's tomatoes take up the most space?

2. Which friend planted equal areas of tomatoes and lettuce?

1. Mole's tomatoes take up the most space.
2. Rabbit planted equal areas of tomatoes and lettuce.

Demitri's Dinner

It's **5:10 p.m.** Demitri the Dragon has guests coming for dinner at **7:30 p.m.**
He plans to prepare the items on these cards. If he does one thing after another,
does he have enough time to make everything before his guests arrive?

Vegetables

14 oz. fresh peas
½ stick butter

Prep time: 14 minutes

Dessert

2 sticks of butter
cake mix
1 cup of milk
eggs
oil

Prep time:
1 hour and 5 minutes

Gravy

1 cube of boullion
1 package of spices
3 tbsp cornstarch
½ cup water

Prep time: 8 minutes

Salad

1 head of iceburg lettuce
½ head of romaine lettuce
1 tomato
2 carrots
2 stalks of celery

Prep time: 10 minutes

Magic Meatloaf

5 pounds of ground beef
1 onion
½ tsp pepper
1 tbsp salt
2 tsp garlic powder
1 can of tomato sauce
1 pound cheddar cheese

Prep time: 40 minutes

Art by Cecilia Messina

He'll be finished with
three minutes to spare.

Racecar Riddles

The race was won by a fraction of a second! To solve
these riddles, use the fractions of the words below.

Where do racecars go to
wash their clothes?

Last ³/₅ of BATHE
First ¹/₂ of LAMP
Last ³/₄ of FUND
Last ¹/₂ of VERY
First ¹/₃ of VET
First ¹/₂ of ROSE
Last ³/₅ of BLOOM

_ _ _ _
_ _ _ _ _ _ _ _
_ _ _ _ _ _ _

What did the hot dog say
when it finished the race first?

Last ¹/₂ of TRIM
First ³/₅ of THEIR
First ¹/₂ of WIND
Last ²/₃ of PEN
Last ¹/₃ of MARKER

" _ ' _   _ _ _ _
_ _ _ _ _ _ _ !"

What will the school for
racecars do after summer?

First ¹/₂ of READ
Last ³/₅ of KAZOO
First ¹/₄ of MAIL

_ _ _ - _ _ _ _ _

Art by Deborah Melman

Where do racecars go to
wash their clothes?
THE LAUNDRY VROOOM

What did the hot dog say when
it finished the race first?
"I'M THE WIENER!"

What will the school for
racecars do after the summer?
RE-ZOOM

Farm Route

This farmer needs to get to his barn. But he can only follow the path with numbers that are divisible by 7. Can you figure out which way the farmer needs to go?

Nighttime Numbers

Can you figure out this number puzzle before bedtime? Place the numbers **1** through **9** in the circles below so that each line of three adds up to **15**.

Place the numbers so that the 5 is in the middle and the other two numbers in each line add up to 10. One way to place them is shown here.

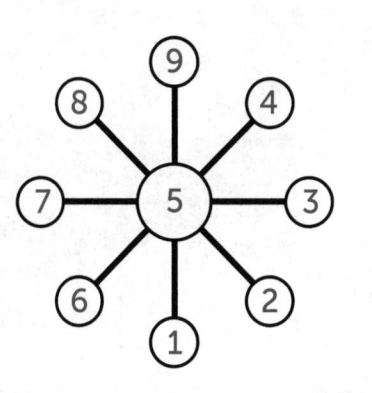

Couch Treasure Hunt

Eli, Owen, Tali, and Theresa found these nine coins under the couch cushions. Use the clues to figure out which coins each sibling found.

HINTS:

- Owen found three of the same coin.
- Eli found the largest coin.
- Theresa found two different coins.
- Tali found 16 cents.

Owen found 3 dimes.
Eli found a quarter.
Theresa found a nickel and a dime.
Tali found a penny, a nickel, and a dime.

Totally!

Gidget Digit loves to play with numbers. Just for fun, she put together these lists. See if you can figure out which list gives you the largest answer. When you've got that, write the colored letters from that list in order in the spaces below to find out the name of Gidget's pet hamster.

1

- Num**B**er of days in Ap**R**il
- Div**I**ded by the number of bears in the Goldilocks story
- Plus the number of le**G**s on a spider
- M**I**nus the number of quar**T**ers in a dollar

TOTAL: _____

2

- Number of vo**W**els (not **I**ncluding Y)
- Multiplie**D** by the number of sides on a penta**G**on
- Plus the number of dim**E**s in two dollars
- Divided by the number of points in a foo**T**ball field goal

TOTAL: _____

3

- Number **O**f states in the USA
- Divided by the numbe**R** of singers in a duet
- Plus the numbe**R** of sides on a decagon
- M**I**nus the number of hour**S** in a day

TOTAL: _____

The name of Gidget's hamster is _ _ _ _ _ _ _ .

Art by Mike Moran

1. 30 ÷ 3 = 10
10 + 8 = 18
18 − 4 = 14

2. 5 × 5 = 25
25 + 20 = 45
45 ÷ 3 = 15

3. 50 ÷ 2 = 25
25 + 10 = 35
35 − 24 = 11

The name of Gidget's hamster is **WIDGET**.

Go Fish

There should be **14** tropical fish swimming through these grids. Using the directions and hints below, can you figure out where all the fish go?

Look at the grids. Each numbered square tells you how many of the empty squares touching it (above, below, left, right, or diagonally) contain a fish. Write an **X** on squares that can't have a fish. Then write an **F** on squares that have a fish.

HINTS:

- A fish cannot go in a square that has a number.

- Put an *X* on all the squares touching a zero.

- Even if you're not sure where to put all the fish connected to a number, fill in the ones you are sure of.

This grid has 4 fish.

	3		1
		1	
			1
		0	

This grid has 10 fish.

			2		
	0				2
		1	4		
	3				
				1	3
3					

Photos by Inusuke/iStock (fish in coral); Burnsboxco/iStock (other fish)

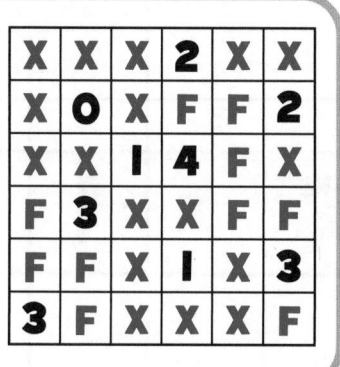

Dive for Five

These divers have a challenge: They must divide this grid into five parts, following the rules below. Can you help them? One shape has been drawn for you. Read the directions and dive in!

RULES:

- Each part consists of five numbers in five squares.

- Each part has a different shape.

- All five numbers in each part add up to 21.

- No part contains two identical numbers.

7	3	3	9	1
1	4	2	5	5
8	8	7	2	4
2	7	7	6	1
1	2	3	3	4

CLICK!

Float Pattern

The numbers on these floats follow a pattern.
Figure out the pattern and then fill in the blanks.

The pattern is +2, +3.
1, 3, 6, 8, 11, 13, 16, 18, 21, 23, 26, 28,
31, 33, 36, 38, 41, 43, 46, 48

Surprise Prize

You've won a prize in the school raffle! But first you have to figure out which item is yours. Follow the clues below to claim your prize!

CLUES:

- The number on your item is not divisible by **5**.
- The number **3** does not appear on your item's tag.
- There are three even digits in your item's number.
- The digits in your prize's number add up to **22**.

The skateboard is the prize.

Dog Addition

Each dog on this page has a value from **1** to **9**. No two dogs have the same value.
Can you use the equations to figure out which number goes with which dog?

 +  =

_____   _____   _____

 + =

_____   _____   _____

 + + =

_____

 + =

_____   _____   _____

 + =

_____   _____   _____

_____

+

_____

+

_____

HINT:  = **3**    = **4**

Art by Mike Moran

3 + 4 = 7; 4 + 4 = 8
3 + 2 + 2 = 7
2 + 6 = 8; 6 + 3 = 9

11	65	53
+22	+12	+46
33	77	99

Lucky Division

Solve these division problems. Then place the letters that represent each number in the spaces below to answer the riddle.

$60 \div 5 = $ **W**

$21 \div 3 = $ **T**

$50 \div 5 = $ **L**

$44 \div 4 = $ **R**

$36 \div 6 = $ **H**

$72 \div 8 = $ **E**

What's at the end of a rainbow?

___ ___ ___ ___ ___ ___ ___ ___ ___ ___
 7   6   9   10 9   7   7   9 11   12

Art by Kevin Zimmer

What's at the end of a rainbow?
THE LETTER W

Lost in the Woods

X marks the spot where you are in the center of this forest. There are a lot of pathways that lead out along even numbered squares. But there is only one path that leads to the edge along only odd-numbered squares. Can you find the path? You may move up, down, left, right, or diagonally.

HINT:
Your first move is to the number **3**. Your last square on your way out of the forest is also the number **3**, in the lower-right-hand corner.

3	2	4	2	9	4	4	8	5
2	8	1	2	8	6	7	6	4
6	5	6	4	6	1	2	9	6
6	1	3	5	8	3	2	1	8
4	9	8	5	X	4	8	7	6
8	2	7	9	8	6	9	2	6
5	2	2	1	6	8	4	7	4
1	4	3	9	2	6	2	5	4
7	6	2	2	6	9	8	6	3

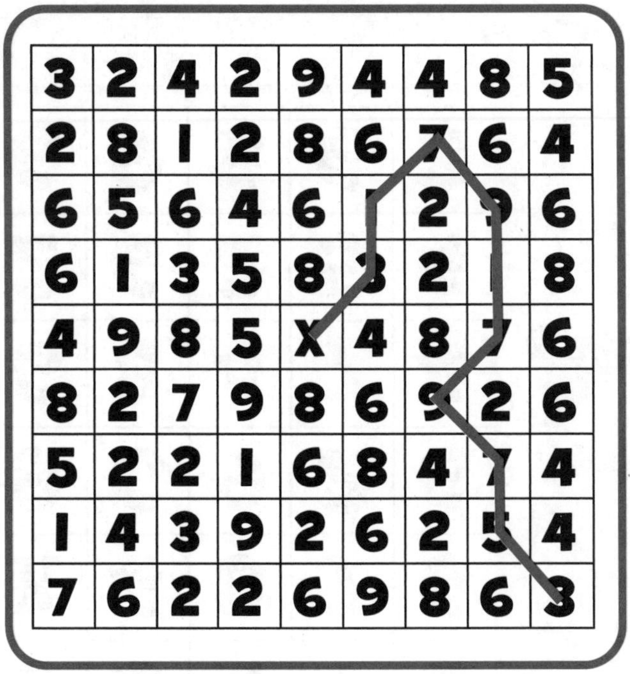

Stevie's Sweets

Stevie used his pocket change to buy some sweets from the bakery.
He spent **$1.08** in all. Afterward, he had one coin left. Which coin?

Art by Brian Michael Weaver

Stevie had one quarter left over.

Sloth-Land Adventure Park

Snoozanne wants to see a concert, Snorbert can't wait to go on a tube tour, and Dozalita is eager to try the ropes course. But all three activities have just started! What time is it?

ROCK-A-BYE CONCERTS
Every 3 hours from 12:00 P.M. to 9:00 P.M.

LAZY RIVER TUBE TOURS
Every 1½ hours from 12:00 P.M. to 9:00 P.M.

TREETOP ROPES COURSE
Every 2 hours from 2:00 P.M. to 8:00 P.M.

It is 6:00 p.m.

Dig This

There should be **13** dog bones buried in this dirt. Using the directions and hints below, can you figure out where all the dog bones go?

Look at the grids. Each numbered square tells you how many of the empty squares touching it (above, below, left, right, or diagonally) contain a dog bone. Write an **X** on squares that can't have a dog bone. Then write **DB** on squares that have a dog bone.

HINTS:

- Put an *X* on all the squares touching a zero.

- Look in the corners where a numbered square may make it more obvious where a bone is buried.

- A bone cannot go in a square that has a number.

This grid has 3 dog bones.

1		0	
2		1	
	2		1

This grid has 10 dog bones.

3		3		3	
					2
2		1			
					2
1		0		3	

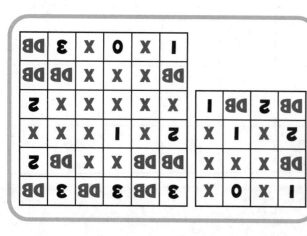

20/20 Vision

Look closely to find all the pairs of numbers next to each other that add up to **20**. These pairs may go across, up, down, or diagonally. Every number will be used as part of one pair.

12	17	3	14	7	16	4
1	8	15	6	13	10	3
19	10	10	5	10	17	12
16	2	9	11	19	8	18
4	7	18	6	1	9	2
13	0	20	14	15	5	11

Art by Don Robison

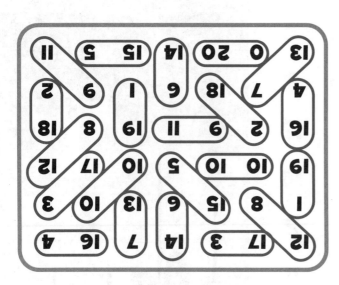

Roller Coaster Pattern

The numbers on these roller coaster cars follow a pattern.
Figure out the pattern and then fill in the blanks.

The numbers go up by 8.
8, 16, 24, 32, 40, 48, 56, 64,
72, 80, 88, 96, 104, 112,
120, 128, 136, 144, 152, 160

Hidden Creature

Cross out each box containing a number that cannot be evenly divided by **9**. Then write down the letters from the remaining boxes. Start with the last letter on the right side of the sixth row and move left. Then write the letters from the fifth row, moving right to left. Do the remaining rows in the same way. You'll find that you've spelled out the name of a dinosaur.

15 V	39 C	54 S	60 F	48 N	24 W
36 P	76 H	19 P	72 O	56 L	88 X
63 T	84 J	21 Y	3 B	90 A	49 K
89 M	81 R	12 D	28 Q	135 E	76 C
42 Y	100 I	27 C	58 F	138 B	72 I
151 Z	64 K	108 R	53 L	162 T	125 N

What's the name of the dinosaur?

___ ___ ___ ___ ___ ___ ___ ___ ___ ___ ___ ___

Art by Kevin Zimmer

		54 S			
36 P			72 O		
63 T				90 A	
	81 R			135 E	
		27 C			72 I
		108 R		162 T	

TRICERATOPS

River Run

Each group of rafters is taking a different route to Camp Pinecone, and each is paddling at a different speed. Can you tell the order in which they will arrive at camp?

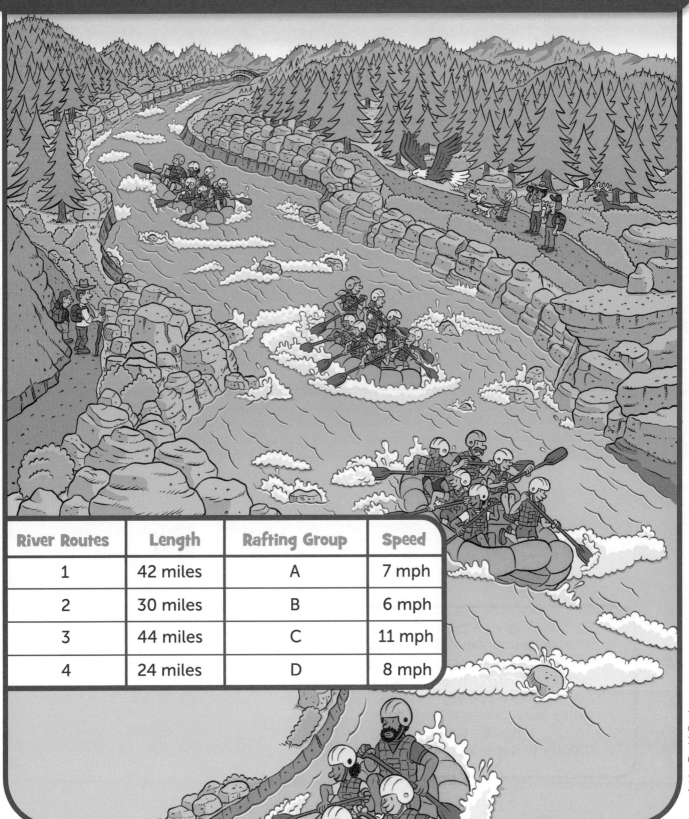

River Routes	Length	Rafting Group	Speed
1	42 miles	A	7 mph
2	30 miles	B	6 mph
3	44 miles	C	11 mph
4	24 miles	D	8 mph

Group D will arrive first in 3 hours.
(24 ÷ 8 = 3)
Group C will arrive second in 4 hours.
(44 ÷ 11 = 4)
Group B will arrive third in 5 hours.
(30 ÷ 6 = 5)
Group A will arrive fourth in 6 hours.
(42 ÷ 7 = 6)

Math Mirth

Do some math, then get a laugh! Use the fractions of the words listed below to solve the two riddles given in this puzzle.

What do math teachers eat?

First ½ of SQUASH
First ⅓ of ARTIST
Last ½ of POEM
Last ½ of CONCEALS

___ ___ ___ ___ ___ ___ ___ ___ ___ ___

Why did the math teacher stop singing karaoke?

Last ³⁄₅ of USHER
Middle ⅓ of MANUAL
Last ½ of CUCUMBER
Middle ⅓ of BEWARE
First ⅓ of SUPERSTAR

___ ___ ___ ___ ___ ___ ___ ___ ___ ___ ___ ___ ___ ___ ___ ___ .

What do math teachers eat?
SQUARE MEALS

Why did the math teacher stop
singing karaoke?
HER NUMBER WAS UP.

Ice-Cream Dreams

It sure is a hot day at Izzy's Ice-Cream Counter. Help Josh, Sammy, Michaela, and Neal sort out their change. Quick, before the ice cream melts!

Josh gave Izzy a $5.00 bill and got 80 cents in change.

How much was his triple-scoop banana split sundae?

Michaela's and Neal's ice-cream cones cost $6.80 together. Michaela received $3.20 in change.

How much money did she give Izzy?

Sammy spent $5.50 on her milkshake and has $2.40 left.

How much did she start with?

Art by Jennifer Zivoin

Josh's ice cream cost $4.20.
Sammy started with $7.90.
Michaela and Neal gave Izzy $10.00.

Stop. Watch. Code.

How much time will it take you to decode these riddles?

CODE

0:00 = **A**	
0:05 = **B**	
0:10 = **C**	
0:15 = **D**	
0:20 = **E**	
0:25 = **F**	
0:30 = **G**	
0:35 = **H**	
0:40 = **I**	
0:45 = **J**	
0:50 = **K**	
0:55 = **L**	
1:00 = **M**	
1:05 = **N**	
1:10 = **O**	
1:15 = **P**	
1:20 = **Q**	
1:25 = **R**	
1:30 = **S**	
1:35 = **T**	
1:40 = **U**	
1:45 = **V**	
1:50 = **W**	
1:55 = **X**	
2:00 = **Y**	
2:05 = **Z**	

I. What time is it when five frogs race to catch one fly?

Answer: 0:25   0:40   1:45   0:20

0:00   0:25   1:35   0:20   1:25

1:10   1:05   0:20.

2. Why shouldn't you stomp on a watch?

Answer: 0:40   1:35 '   1:30   0:00

1:50   0:00   1:30   1:35   0:20

1:10   0:25   1:35   0:40   1:00   0:20.

3. What goes ticktock, ticktock and hides in a lake in Scotland?

Answer: 1:35   0:35   0:20

0:10   0:55   1:10   0:10   0:50

1:05   0:20   1:30   1:30

1:00   1:10   1:05   1:30   1:35   0:20   1:25.

What time is it when...?

ZaP!

Art by Mike Dammer

1. Five after one
2. It's a waste of time.
3. The Clock Ness Monster

Follow the Flakes

Can you find a path from START to FINISH that adds up to **21**? You can move across, up, down, or diagonally from one snowflake to the next.

START

3	6	3	7
0	4	2	5
5	3	6	0
2	1	0	2

FINISH

How Old Is Olivia?

Today is Olivia's birthday! Use the clues below to figure out how old she is.

CLUES:

- Olivia's sister, Bella, is **13** years old.

- Olivia is five years younger than her brother Jayden and three years older than her brother Luis.

- Luis is six years younger than Bella.

Art by Jamie Smith

Olivia is 10 years old.

Umbrella Fun

Black out the squares listed for each row. When you're done, the remaining letters will spell out the answer to the riddle.

- **Row A:** Black out **3**.
- **Row B:** Black out **1** and **4**.
- **Row C:** Black out **2** and **5**.
- **Row D:** Black out **1**, **3**, and **4**.
- **Row E:** Black out **2** and **5**.

	1	2	3	4	5
A	W	H	O	E	N
B	C	T	H	O	E
C	S	E	U	N	T
D	R	I	T	P	S
E	O	L	U	T	D

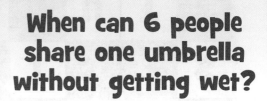

When can 6 people share one umbrella without getting wet?

__ __ __ __

__ __ __

__ __ __ __

__ __ __

	1	2	3	4	5
A	W	H		E	N
B		T	H		E
C	S		U	N	
D		I			S
E	O		U	T	

When can 6 people share one
umbrella without getting wet?
WHEN THE SUN IS OUT

Let It Snow

There should be **14** snowflakes on these mittens. Using the directions and hints below, can you figure out where all the snowflakes go?

Look at the grids. Each numbered square tells you how many of the empty squares touching it (above, below, left, right, or diagonally) contain a snowflake. Write an **X** on squares that can't have a snowflake. Then write an **S** on squares that have a snowflake.

This grid has 4 snowflakes.

		3	
3			
	1		0

This grid has 10 snowflakes.

	2			1	
				3	
	5			4	
	2		1		0

Photo by © Siede Preis/Exactostock/SuperStock

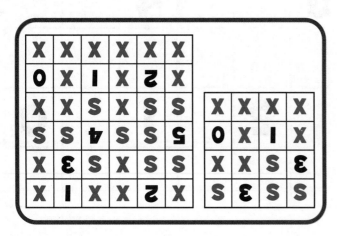

Perfect Pairs

Some things make the perfect pair! Every number in the grid below can be paired with one other number. The key to finding the pairs is to look for those numbers that have a difference of **9** when the smaller number is subtracted from the larger. Pairs can be grouped across, up, down, backward, or diagonally.

65	57	66	98	107	100
58	74	72	108	87	91
49	81	80	89	99	78
105	67	75	101	110	68
76	96	84	94	102	77
83	92	103	95	86	93

Art by Laura Watson

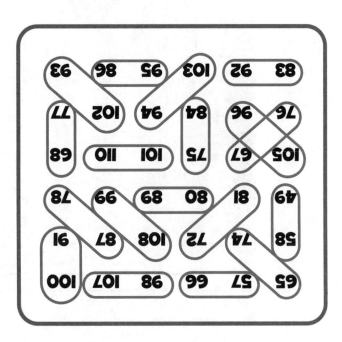

Petal Patterns

The numbers in each set of flowers follow a pattern. Can you find the patterns and figure out which numbers are missing?

A. 14, 6
B. 21, 6
C. 10, 8

Fish, Fruit, and Feathers

A fish mystery, a fruit brainteaser, and a penguin puzzle—use your math skills to figure out the three mini challenges below.

FRUIT FIGURES

Each type of fruit represents a certain number. Look at the equations to figure out which number each fruit represents.

$$1 + 4 = \text{(pear)}$$

$$\text{(pear)} + \text{(pear)} = \text{(lemon)}$$

$$\text{(pear)} - \text{(apple)} = 2$$

$$\text{(apple)} + \text{(blueberry)} = \text{(lemon)}$$

REEL IT IN

Lyla is spending the day fishing with her family. Her line can hold only **6** pounds. Which fish can she catch? (Hint: **1** pound = **16** ounces.)

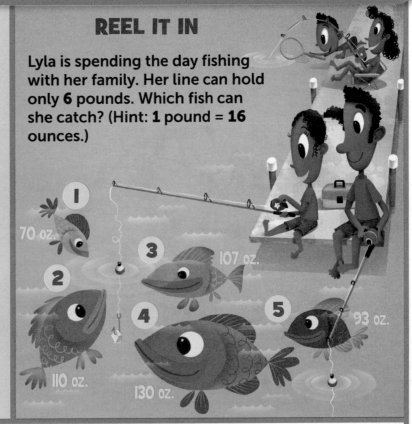

1 — 70 oz.
3 — 107 oz.
2 — 110 oz.
4 — 130 oz.
5 — 93 oz.

PENGUIN PUZZLER

It's lunchtime, but Ben can't get to his lunchbox. He has forgotten his locker combination! Luckily, he remembers some clues that might help. Using the clues, can you figure out the three numbers in Ben's locker combination?

CLUES:

- The first number equals the number of months in a year.

- The second number falls halfway between the first and last numbers.

- The last number is double the first number.

COOL AS ICE

Art by Pat Lewis (Fruit Figures); Kevin Zimmer (Reel It In); and Jason Tharp (Penguin Puzzler)

FRUIT FIGURES
Pear = 5, Lemon = 10, Apple = 3,
Orange = 7

REEL IT IN
Lyla can catch #1 or #5.

PENGUIN PUZZLER
Ben's locker combination is 12, 18, 24.

BONUS
AN ICEBERG-ER

Ten Out of Ten

To solve the riddle below, check the fraction underneath each blank space. The fractions tell you which of the ten letters written on the barn to use, going from left to right. Keep filling in the blanks with the correct letters until the answer is revealed.

ACEINOPRST

What did the sign on the chicken coop say?

$\frac{8}{10}$ $\frac{6}{10}$ $\frac{6}{10}$ $\frac{9}{10}$ $\frac{10}{10}$ $\frac{4}{10}$ $\frac{5}{10}$ $\frac{7}{10}$ $\frac{3}{10}$ $\frac{1}{10}$ $\frac{2}{10}$ $\frac{3}{10}$

What did the sign on
the chicken coop say?
ROOST IN PEACE

Thanksgiving Tidbits

Marielle and Kelson are helping their mom bake an apple pie to bring to Grandma's. But first they have to buy the ingredients. Look at the recipe on the sign and find all the items on it. How much money will all the ingredients cost?

Art by Diane Palmisciano

The ingredients cost $10.75.

Truck Tunes

Use the number pairs underneath the blanks at the bottom to solve the riddle on this page.
Start at **0** and move to the right to the first number, then up to the second number.

What do long-distance truckers listen to?

◯◯◯◯◯ - ◯◯◯◯◯◯◯ ◯◯◯◯◯

1,7 4,2 2,5 8,6 5,4   9,9 7,3 4,8 6,6 2,3 4,2 7,8   3,6 9,2 8,6 3,9 1,7

What do long-distance
truckers listen to?
CROSS-COUNTRY MUSIC

Calendar Clues

Spike, Terry, and Rex love throwing birthday parties. When do they get to celebrate their birthdays? Use the clues below to figure out the day on which each of them was born, as well as their current ages.

Terry: My birthday is midway between Groundhog Day and Valentine's Day. Next year, my age will match the day of the month on which I was born.

Rex: I was born in the last month of the year. The day is the one in the middle of the month. My birth year came two years before Terry's.

Spike: I was born in a month that has one *E* and no *R* in its name. The day falls three weeks before the last day of the month. I was born four years before Rex.

Spike: June 9, 13 years old
Terry: December 16, 9 years old
Rex: February 8, 7 years old

Top It Off

There should be **14** pepperoni on these pizzas. Using the directions and hints below, can you figure out where all the pepperoni go?

Look at the grids. Each numbered square tells you how many of the empty squares touching it (above, below, left, right, or diagonally) contain a pepperoni. Write an **X** on squares that can't have a pepperoni. Then write a **P** on squares that have a pepperoni.

HINTS:

• Put an *X* on all the squares touching a zero.

• Look in the corners where a numbered square may make it more obvious where a slice of pepperoni belongs.

• Pepperoni cannot go in a square that has a number.

This grid has 4 pepperoni.

2			0
	4		
0			2

This grid has 10 pepperoni.

0					1
	1		5		
		3			2
	1		5		
				4	
	0				2

Photos by © imageBROKER/SuperStock (pizza); © Brand X Pictures/Exactostock/SuperStock (pizza box)

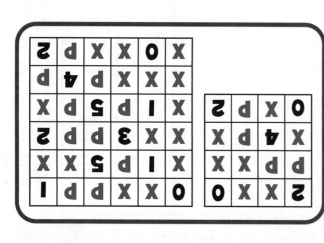

Apples All Around

In every row of these apple trees—down, across, and diagonally—there are **30** apples. We've provided the number of apples in each corner tree. Can you use these numbers to figure out how many apples are in the other trees?

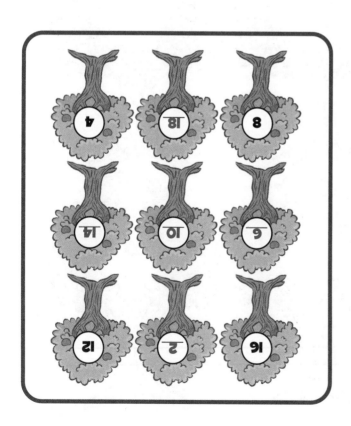

Cat Addition

Each cat on this page has a value from **1** to **9**. No two cats have the same value.
Can you use the equations to figure out which number goes with which cat?

 + =

_____ _____ _____

 + =

_____ _____ _____

 + +  =

_____ _____ _____ _____

 + =

_____ _____ _____

 + =

_____ _____ _____

_____

+

_____

_____

+

_____

_____

+

_____

HINT: = 5   = 7

5 + 2 = 7; 1 + 1 = 2
2 + 1 + 1 = 4
4 + 3 = 7; 3 + 5 = 8

11	32	12
+88	+35	+36
99	67	48

Leap Frog

Freddy the frog is feeling pretty even-tempered today. Help him hop across the pond by moving up or down, left or right, but only to the even numbers.

62	20	31	55	96	66	36	56	16
44	60	2	94	98	21	47	53	76
17	56	51	37	10	6	70	13	57
9	38	41	8	85	43	72	69	39
22	24	45	80	74	49	40	86	64
28	61	19	33	92	95	32	23	12
30	36	42	18	66	11	16	35	71

START

FINISH

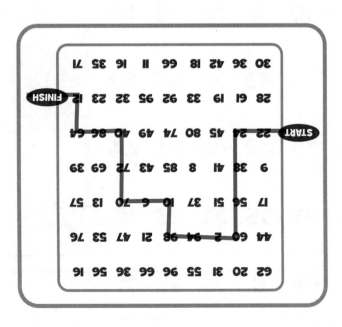

Trip to the Market

Margot and Nina spent **$4.00** on four items at the farmers' market.
Can you use the clues to figure out which four items they bought?

Item 1 is labeled "fresh," is not a baked good, and costs $0.50.

Item 2 is not in a basket, is not sold by the slice, and costs $1.00.

Item 3 is not a baked good, is not labeled "fresh," and costs $0.50.

Item 4 is labeled "fresh," is not sold by the dozen, and costs the
remainder of their spending money.

Item 1: Apple
Item 2: Brownie
Item 3: Pickle
Item 4: Lettuce

If at First . . .

The answer to the riddle below is easy if you know your measurements. Each "if" statement will give you a letter and tell you where to put it. Fill in all the letters and you will have your answer—no ifs, ands, or buts!

1. If a tablespoon is larger than a teaspoon, the first letter is a **C**. If not, it is a **D**.

2. If there are 36 inches in a yard, the second and ninth letters are **O**. If not they are **A**.

3. If there are two pints in a quart, the tenth letter is a **U**. If not, the fifth letter is a **U**.

4. If there are 6,000 feet in a mile, letters 3, 4, and 8 are **T**. If not, they are **L**.

5. If there are 1,000 meters in a kilometer, letter 11 is an **R**. If not, it is an **S**.

6. If a millimeter is smaller than a centimeter, the sixth letter is an **E**. If not it is an **R**.

7. If a ton is more than 1,000 pounds, the seventh letter is an **F**. If not, it is a **B**.

8. If a meter is longer than a foot, the fifth letter is an **I**. If not, the tenth letter is an **I**.

What do you call dough used for making dog biscuits?

___ ___ ___ ___ ___ ___   ___ ___ ___ ___ ___
1   2   3   4   5   6   7   8   9   10 11

Art by Kelly Kennedy

Order in the Court!

Judge J. J. Jones Jr. is presiding over another case. Help her get order in her courtroom by figuring out what number comes next in each series. Hurry, before she has to pound her gavel again!

A 1, 8, 15, 22, __29__

B 36, 30, 24, 18, _____

C 64, 32, 16, 8, _____

D 3, 9, 27, _____

E 4, 17, 30, 43, _____

F 81, 72, 63, _____

G 256, 64, 16, _____

H 5, 25, 125, _____

I 12, 34, 56, _____

J 1, 4, 9, 16, _____

K 2, 12, 20, 21, 22, _____

L 12, 6, 18, 12, 24, _____

M 12, 23, 34, 45, _____

N 3, 6, 33, 36, 63, _____

O 20, 25, 22, 27, 24, _____

P 9, 36, 12, 48, _____

Q 9, 6, 12, 9, 15, _____

R 40, 10, 60, 15, _____

A. 29 Keep adding 7
B. 12 Keep subtracting 6
C. 4 Keep dividing by 2
D. 81 Keep multiplying by 3
E. 56 Keep adding 13
F. 54 Keep subtracting 9
G. 4 Keep dividing by 4
H. 625 Keep multiplying by 5
I. 78 Write the numbers 1 through 8 as two-digit numbers
J. 25 Numbers are the squares of 1, 2, 3, 4, 5
K. 23 Numbers that have a 2 in ascending order
L. 18 Numbers go down 6 and then up 12
M. 56 Numbers in 1s place increase by 1
Numbers in 10s place increase by 1
N. 66 Numbers made up only of 3s and 6s in ascending order
O. 29 Add 5 and then subtract 3
P. 16 Multiply by 4 and then divide by 3
Q. 12 Subtract 3 and then add 6
R. 90 Divide by 4 then multiply by 6

Creepy-Crawly Calculations

To solve the riddle, use the fractions of the words
below. The first one has been done for you.

1. Last ⅓ of LOCUST
2. Last ⅛ of MOSQUITO
3. Last ¼ of WASP

4. Last ½ of BEDBUG
5. Last ⅙ of EARWIG
6. First ¼ of INCHWORM

7. Last ¼ of SLUG
8. First ⅙ of MANTIS
9. Last ⅓ of BEE

What did the itchy dog say to the flea?

ST_ _ _ _ _ _ _ _ _ _ _ _ _!

What did the itchy dog say to the flea?
STOP BUGGING ME!

Pick a Number

Three numbers are above each set of statements. See if you can fill in the blanks with these numbers so that the sentences make sense.

26 28 9

Bobbi played _____ holes of miniature golf with her father. His score was _____ , but Bobbi won with a score of _____ .

20 22 35

Jack scored _____ points for his basketball team. Unfortunately, they still lost. The score was _____ to _____ .

118 23 6

I checked _____ books out of the library today. One of them has _____ pages. They are due back on April _____ rd.

9, 28, 26

20, 35, 22

6, 118, 23

Toys for Twins

Nate and Jada want to buy presents for their younger twin brothers. They bought four toys from the store window and paid **$13.20** with their allowance money. Which four toys did they buy?

$5.25

$7.50

500 PIECES!

$1.75

$3.25

Magic KiT

$4.40

$3.50

$4.20

$2.00

$5.10

Nate and Jada bought the airplane, paints, puzzle, and dump truck for $13.20.

Answer Hunt

Go on the prowl for the answers to these clues. (Some clues ask for word answers. Others ask for number answers.) Write the answers on the numbered blanks. Then take each letter from its blank and put it into the matching numbered square on the grid. When you are done, read from left to right to find a number-related fact.

A. 2 + 2 + 2 + 2 + 2 + 2 + 2:

___ ___ ___ ___ ___ ___ ___ ___
27 35 19 42 2 53 23 12

B. Ice or roller:

___ ___ ___ ___ ___
24 5 4 43 45

C. Number after 999,999 (2 words):

___ ___ ___   ___ ___ ___ ___ ___ ___ ___
48 31 9   18 41 52 22 51 17 46

D. Definitely needed, I ____ have that:

___ ___ ___ ___
50 33 7 13

E. 6 + 5 + 4 + 3 + 2:

___ ___ ___ ___ ___ ___
3 16 11 36 47 38

F. Person in charge of a project or job:

___ ___ ___ ___
32 26 20 49

G. 90 ÷ 3:

___ ___ ___ ___ ___ ___
34 40 1 28 15 14

H. The price of something:

___ ___ ___ ___
21 29 8 39

I. 48 − 36:

___ ___ ___ ___ ___ ___
25 30 6 37 10 44

HINT:
For clues with number answers, spell out the number rather than using numerals. For instance, spell out "eleven" rather than writing "11."

1	2		3	4	5	6	7
	8	9	10	11	12	13	14
—	15	16	17		18	19	20
21	22	23	24		25	26	
27	28	29	30	31		32	33
34		35	36	37	38		39
40	41	42	43	44	45	46	
47	48		49	50	51	52	53

A. FOURTEEN
B. SKATE
C. ONE MILLION
D. MUST
E. TWENTY
F. BOSS
G. THIRTY
H. COST
I. TWELVE

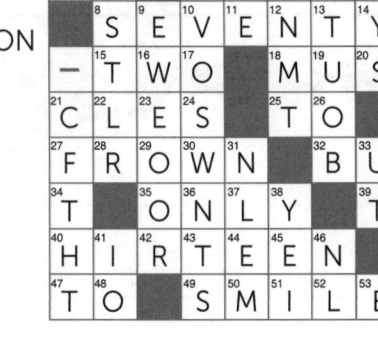

It takes seventy-two muscles to frown
but only thirteen to smile.

Web Search

There should be **13** spiders on this web. Using the directions and hints below, can you figure out where all the spiders go?

Look at the grids. Each numbered square tells you how many of the empty squares touching it (above, below, left, right, or diagonally) contain a spider. Write an **X** on squares that can't have a spider. Then write an **S** on squares that have a spider.

HINTS:

- Put an *X* on all the squares touching a zero.

- Look in the corners where a numbered square may make it more obvious where a spider is hiding.

- A spider cannot go in a square that has a number.

This grid has 3 spiders.

	1		2
0			
	2	2	2

This grid has 10 spiders.

3		2		2
				3
0			4	
				3
1		1		2

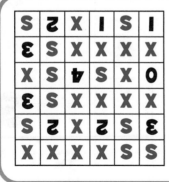

Sum Circles

Place a number from **1** to **10** in each of the yellow circles. In each case, the number in the green section where two circles overlap is the sum of the two yellow circles forming the overlap. No two circles can have the same number. (We've placed the first number for you.)

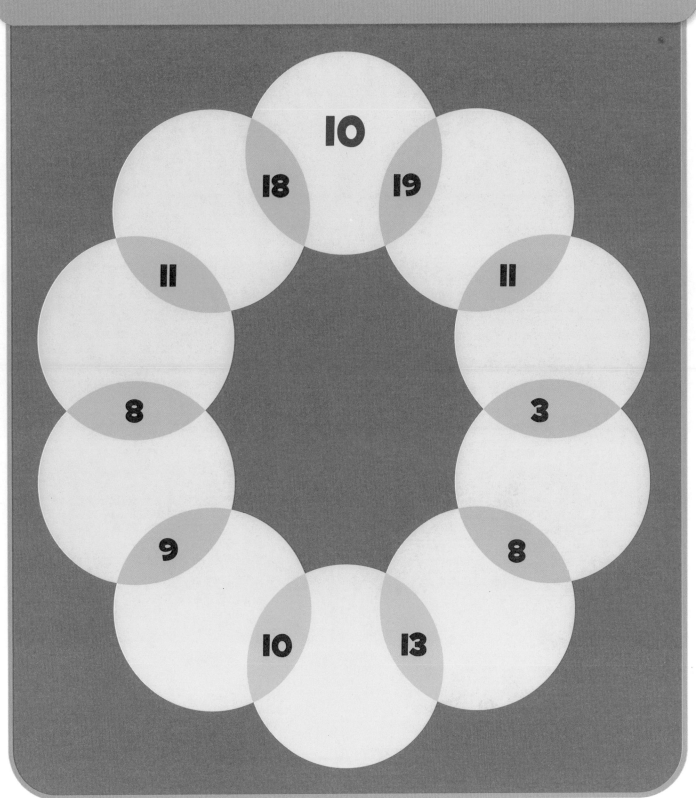

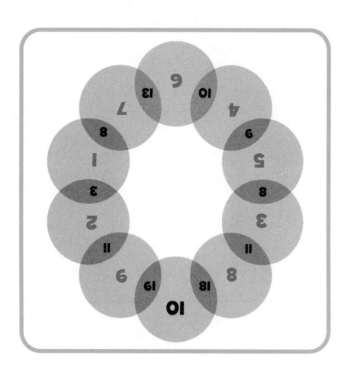

Hoop Heights

Here is the starting lineup for the Central School Eagles. Using the clues, can you give the height in feet and inches for each player?

CLUES:

- Rory is 61 inches tall.
- Judy and Rafi are the same height.
- Shelly is an inch taller than Rafi.
- Max is between Rory and Shelly.
- Judy is 3 inches shorter than Rory.

STARTING LINEUP

Player	Height
Rory	_____
Judy	_____
Rafi	_____
Shelly	_____
Max	_____

Art by Rafa Alvarez

Rory: 5'1"
Judy: 4'10"
Rafi: 4'10"
Shelly: 4'11"
Max: 5'0"

Funny Fractions

To solve the riddle, use the fractions of words listed below. The first one has been done for you.

First ²/₅ of HINGE

Last ³/₄ of IDEA

Last ½ of SAND

First ²/₅ of GLASS

First ²/₃ of OWL

First ¹/₅ of SHAKE

Last ³/₄ of WEEK

What is a firefly's favorite game?

H I __ __ - __ __ __ - __ __ __ __ - __ __ __ __

What is a firefly's favorite game?
HIDE-AND-GLOW-SEEK

Food for Thought

This menu is missing something. Can you fill in the missing prices by finding the different number pattern for each section?

Sandwiches

Cheese............................$2.00
BLT.................................$_____
Tuna...............................$2.50
Roast Beef....................$2.75
Super Club....................$3.00

From the Grill

Hamburger....................$2.50
Eggs and Bacon.............$2.30
Steak..............................$2.60
Foot-Long Hot Dog......$_____
Fried Chicken................$2.70

Side Orders

French Fries...................$1.00
Onion Rings..................$0.75
Cole Slaw......................$1.50
Salad..............................$1.25
Soup...............................$_____

Desserts

Pie..................................$_____
Sundae...........................$1.13
Cake................................$1.01
Big Cookie.....................$0.89
Raisin Bar......................$0.77

Sandwiches	$2.25 (+$.25)
From the Grill	$2.40 (−$.20, +$.30)
Side Orders	$2.00 (−$.25, +$.75)
Desserts	$1.25 (−$.12)

Throw Me a Bone

Cross out all the boxes in which the number can be evenly divided by **3**. Then write the remaining letters in the spaces below to spell the answer to the riddle.

10	33	25	12	23	13	66	41	37	6	11
T	Z	H	U	E	Y	I	C	A	K	N
42	17	4	21	60	28	26	24	5	29	38
P	T	A	M	X	F	F	J	O	R	D
10	9	19	90	16	41	3	62	27	14	50
N	L	E	Q	W	O	B	N	V	E	S

Why do museums have old dinosaur bones?

___ ___ ___ ___ ' ___

___ ___ ___ ___ ___.

Art by Alec Longstreth

Why do museums have
old dinosaur bones?
THEY CAN'T AFFORD
NEW ONES.

Pia's Piggy Bank

Pia has been saving up her allowance for something special—a stuffed animal! When she emptied her piggy bank the other day to count her earnings, she found a bunch of coins—and a riddle for you to solve! Can you use the clues below to figure out how many of each type of coin Pia had in her piggy bank?

CLUES:

- Pia's piggy bank had quarters, dimes, nickels, and pennies.

- When she added up the coins, they totaled **$4.92**.

- Pia noticed that she had the same number of each type of coin.

Pia had 12 quarters, 12 dimes, 12 nickels, and 12 pennies.

Chip In

There should be **12** chocolate chips on these cookies. Using the directions and hints below, can you figure out where all the chocolate chips go?

Look at the grids. Each numbered square tells you how many of the empty squares touching it (above, below, left, right, or diagonally) contain a chocolate chip. Write an **X** on squares that can't have a chocolate chip. Then write **CC** on squares that have a chocolate chip.

HINTS:

- Put an *X* on all the squares touching a zero.

- Look in the corners where a numbered square may make it more obvious where a chocolate chip is hiding.

- A chocolate chip cannot go in a square that has number.

This grid has 2 chocolate chips.

This grid has 10 chocolate chips.

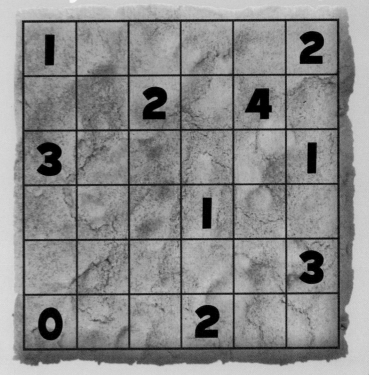

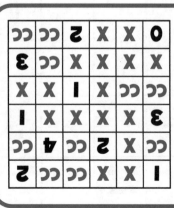

Find Fifty

All the rows except one, and all the columns except one, have numbers that add up to **50**. Can you find the one row and one column whose numbers *don't* add up to **50**?

10	6	4	2	10	10	8
6	4	10	10	9	1	10
1	10	6	4	10	9	10
10	8	10	10	10	7	3
4	10	9	6	1	10	10
10	2	10	8	3	10	7
9	10	1	10	7	3	10

10	3	7	10	1	10	9
7	10	3	8	10	2	10
10	10	1	6	10	9	4
3	7	10	10	10	8	10
10	6	4	10	9	1	
10	1	9	10	10	4	6
8	10	2	4	6	10	

Candy Counter

Each piece of colorful candy costs less than ten cents. Can you look at these equations and figure out the price of each kind?

🍬 + 🍬 + 🍬 + 🍬 = 16¢

⬛ − ⬛ + 3¢ = ⬛

36¢ − 🌽 − 🌽 − 🌽 = 🌽

10¢ + 🍬 + 🍬 − 🍬 = 15¢

18¢ − ⦿ − ⦿ − ⦿ − ⦿ = 14¢

🍭 + 🍭 + 6¢ = 12¢ − 🍭

🍫 + 🍫 + 🍫 − 4¢ = 8¢ + 🍫

$$4 + 4 + 4 + 4 = 16$$
$$3 - 3 + 3 = 3$$
$$36 - 9 - 9 - 9 = 9$$
$$10 + 5 + 5 - 5 = 15$$
$$18 - 1 - 1 - 1 - 1 = 14$$
$$2 + 2 + 6 = 12 - 2$$
$$6 + 6 + 6 - 4 = 8 + 6$$

Monty's Muscles

Monty is making muscles. He can choose from six different weight amounts to create barbells that weigh from **18** to **56** pounds. Can you come up with the right combinations of weights to complete Monty's workout? Monty will never use more than one plate of any weight at a time.

Monty's Weight Plate Options

18 Pounds

12 Pounds

16 Pounds

15 Pounds

10 Pounds

8 Pounds

1. **18** pounds—**2** weights

2. **27** pounds—**2** weights

3. **30** pounds—**2** weights

4. **35** pounds—**3** weights

5. **33** pounds—**2** weights

6. **46** pounds—**3** weights

7. **39** pounds—**3** weights

8. **56** pounds—**4** weights

1. 8 + 10 = 18 pounds

2. 12 + 15 = 27 pounds

3. 12 + 18 = 30 pounds

4. 8 + 12 + 15 = 35 pounds

5. 15 + 18 = 33 pounds

6. 12 + 16 + 18 = 46 pounds

7. 8 + 15 + 16 = 39 pounds

8. 10 + 12 + 16 + 18 = 56 pounds

Totally!

Gidget Digit loves numbers. Just for fun, she put together these lists. See if you can figure out which list gives you the largest answer. When you've got that, write the shaded letters from that list in order in the spaces below to find out what Gidget's favorite season is.

1

- Number of tentacles on **A**n octop**U**s
- Multiplied by **T**he number of babies in a set of q**U**intuplets
- Divided by the number of di**M**es in a dollar
- Plus the **N**umber of cups in a pint

TOTAL: _____

2

- Number of kittens **W**ho lost their m**I**ttens
- Plus the **N**umber of hours in **T**wo days
- Plus the number of p**E**riods in a regular hockey game
- Minus the number of yea**R**s in half a century

TOTAL: _____

3

- Number of day**S** in December
- Min**U**s the nu**M**ber of nickels in a quarter
- Plus the nu**M**ber of singers in a quartet
- Divided by th**E** numbe**R** of bases in baseball, not including home plate

TOTAL: _____

Gidget's favorite season is _____ .

Art by Mike Moran

1. 8 × 5 = 40
40 ÷ 10 = 4
4 + 2 = 6

2. 3 + 48 = 51
51 + 3 = 54
54 − 50 = 4

3. 31 − 5 = 26
6 + 4 = 30
30 ÷ 3 = 10

Gidget's favorite seasons is **SUMMER**.

Go Like Sixty

Work your way through this maze from START to FINISH. You're allowed to pass only through numbers that are factors of **60**. (A factor is a number that divides evenly into a larger number, leaving no remainder.)

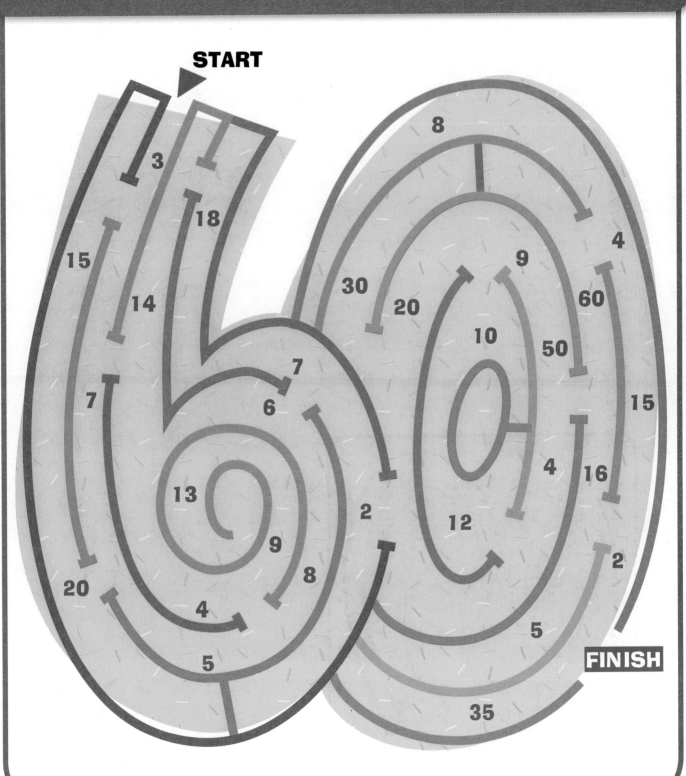

START

FINISH

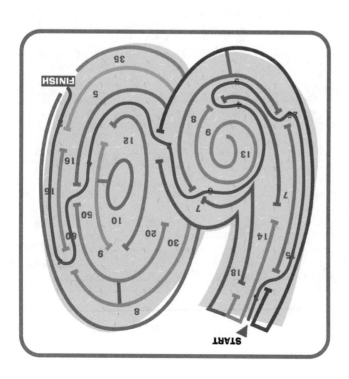

Planet Zlippo's Blippos

Creatures called Blippos live on Planet Zlippo. When it rains, each Blippo splits into **2** every hour. When it snows, each Blippo splits into **3** every hour. Read a weather report for Planet Zlippo from last week. Then figure out how the weather affected the number of Blippos in the space garden.

Last Friday on Planet Zlippo, it rained for **6** hours. Before the rain began, there was only **1** Blippo in the space garden. How many were in the garden after the rain stopped? How many would have ended up in the garden if it had snowed instead?

BONUS
Are there more Blippos with polka dots or without polka dots in this picture?

Art by Joe Rocco

There were 64 Blippos in the space garden after the rain. If it had snowed, there would have been 729 Blippos in the space garden.

BONUS
There are more Blippos without polka dots.

Nap Time for Trolls

Three trolls live under the bridge. The people of Tilly Town want to cross the bridge when all three trolls are napping. Starting at **8:00 a.m.**, each troll repeats a sleeping pattern. (See below.) At what time can the townspeople cross?

BONUS
Find **5** things in the scene that rhyme with *troll*.

Huff Troll
Awake for one hour, sleeps for two hours

Ruff Troll
Sleeps two hours, awake for one hour

Tuff Troll
Sleeps one hour, up for three hours

Art by Gina Perry

The townspeople can cross the bridge between 12:00 p.m. and 1:00 p.m. when all three trolls are asleep.

BONUS
We found: bowl, roll, hole, mole, and fishing pole. You may have found others.

What's for Dessert?

This menu features sweet treats—and delicious riddles! To solve the riddles, look at the numbered blanks. The first number under each blank tells you which menu item to look at; the second tells you which letter in that item to use. For example, the first one is **1-3**. The 1 tells you to go to PEACH PIE. Count 3 letters in, and you've got an A. Fill in the rest of the letters to get all the riddle answers.

Dessert Menu

1. PEACH PIE
2. KEY LIME PIE
3. BANANA SPLIT
4. LEMON PUDDING
5. MISSISSIPPI MUD PIE
6. SEVEN-LAYER CAKE
7. BLUEBERRY COBBLER
8. DOUBLE-FUDGE BROWNIE
9. WHITE-CHOCOLATE MOUSSE

What's the best thing to eat in a bathtub?

A __ __ __ __ __ __ __ __ __ __ __
1-3   3-7   1-1   4-4   3-5 4-12 2-2   1-4   3-4   2-1   4-2

Why do doughnuts go to the dentist?

__ __ __ __ __
9-4 4-4   8-10 2-2   3-11

__ __ __ __ __ __ __ __
8-7   5-2   2-4   4-1   9-3   4-5   8-10   3-7

Who serves ice cream faster than a speeding bullet?

__ __ __ __ __ __ __ __ __ __ !
6-1   1-4   4-4   8-2   4-6   7-4   6-10 4-3   3-4   6-5

Art by Peter Grosshauser

What's the best thing to
eat in a bathtub?
A SPONGE CAKE

Why do doughnuts go to the dentist?
TO GET FILLINGS

Who serves ice cream faster than a
speeding bullet?
SCOOPERMAN!

Nest Quest

There should be **14** eggs in these nests. Using the directions and hints below, can you figure out where all the eggs go?

Look at the grids. Each numbered square tells you how many of the empty squares touching it (above, below, left, right, or diagonally) contain an egg. Write an **X** on squares that can't have an egg. Then write an **E** on squares that have an egg.

HINTS:

- An egg cannot go in a square that has a number.

- In both grids, start by putting an *X* in all four of the squares touching the zero square. That will give you three squares to put in eggs that are around the square numbered 3.

- Remember that eggs can only go in squares that touch a numbered square.

This grid has 4 eggs.

	1	0	
3		2	
	2		1

This grid has 10 eggs.

		1		1
4				
		2		2
4		3		
		2		3
2				0

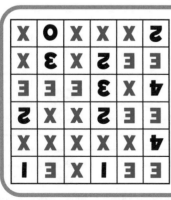

Star Power

Help these stars really shine. Fill in each star with one of the numbers from **1** to **19**. The three stars that make up the side of each triangle should total **22**. No number will appear more than once. We've put in a few numbers to start you off. Fill in the rest, and you are a stellar solver!

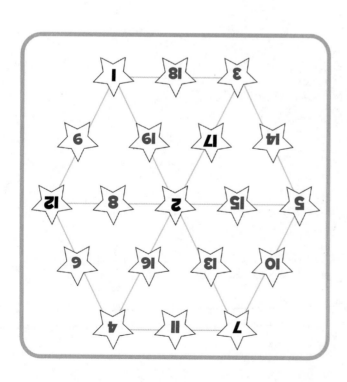

Winning Number

Somewhere in this picture is the winner of this year's Numerical Marathon.
Use these clues to figure out the number of the runner who won the race.

CLUES:

- The sum of the two digits is either **7** or **8**.

- If you switch the order of the digits, the new number would be **27** greater than it is now.

Runner 25 won the race.

Drop Everything

To solve the riddle below, solve each math problem. Then find the raindrop with the matching number. Place the letter in that raindrop in the space next to the math problem. Read down the letters to get your answer.

Raindrops (top row): Z 23 · I 18 · T 16 · W 15 · K 12 · E 20 · C O

Raindrops (bottom row): N 11 · A 24 · R 35 · A 24 · R 35 · H 6 · S 9

How does a weather forecaster pay her bills?

Problem	Number	Letter
5 × 3 =	_____	_____
2 × 9 =	_____	_____
4 × 4 =	_____	_____
6 × 1 =	_____	_____
7 × 5 =	_____	_____
3 × 8 =	_____	_____
6 × 3 =	_____	_____
11 × 1 =	_____	_____
17 × 0 =	_____	_____
2 × 3 =	_____	_____
5 × 4 =	_____	_____
8 × 0 =	_____	_____
4 × 3 =	_____	_____
9 × 1 =	_____	_____

Art by Larisa Lauber

How does a weather
forecaster pay her bills?
WITH RAIN CHECKS

One Time Only

Can you fill in the blanks in these equations with the numbers from **0** to **9**? Each number will be used only once. Here's a clue to help you get started: Number **6** is used in equation "E."

A. ____ + ____ = 14

B. ____ × ____ = 12

C. ____ + ____ = 10

D. ____ + ____ = 8

E. ____ + ____ = 6

A. 9 + 5 = 14
B. 4 × 3 = 12
C. 2 + 8 = 10
D. 1 + 7 = 8
E. 0 + 6 = 6

Bird Addition

Each bird on this page has a value from **1** to **9**. No two birds have the same value. Can you use the equations to figure out which number goes with which bird?

  =

_____ _____ _____

 + =

_____ _____ _____

 +

_____ _____

 + =

_____ _____ _____

 + =

_____ _____ _____

 + =

_____ _____ _____

+ _____ + _____ + _____

_____ _____ _____

HINT: = 1   = 5

Art by Mike Moran

1 + 4 = 5; 2 + 2 = 4
3 + 1 + 1 = 5
4 + 4 = 8; 3 + 4 = 7

11	24	65
+87	+42	+13
98	66	78

Library Logic

Lucy, Luther, and Lawrence left the library with a lot of books! How many books did they each check out? Read the clues below to solve this puzzle.

CLUES:

- Together, they took out **18** library books.

- Lucy took out two more books than Luther.

- Luther took out two more books than Lawrence.

Lucy took out 8 books, Luther took out
6 books, and Lawrence took out 4 books.